Choosing
Your
Apprenticeship

Caroline Barker

Choosing Your Apprenticeship

This first edition published in 2011 by Trotman Publishing, a division of Crimson Publishing Ltd,
Westminster House, Kew Road, Richmond, Surrey TW9 2ND.

© Trotman Publishing 2011

Author: Caroline Barker

The right of Caroline Barker to be identified as the author of this work has been asserted by her in
accordance with the Copyright, Designs and Patents Act, 1988.

British Library Cataloguing in Publication Data
A catalogue record for this book is available from the British Library
ISBN 978 1 84455 388 4

Typeset by RefineCatch Ltd, Bungay, Suffolk.

Printed and bound in the UK by Ashford Colour Press, Gosport, Hants.

Contents

PART TWO: DIRECTORY OF APPRENTICESHIPS

PART THREE: END NOTE

About the author

Caroline Barker is a professionally qualified careers advisor with many years' experience in providing guidance and counselling to a wide range of clients. She has worked with school pupils, apprenticeship trainees, college students and adults seeking a career change. Her work at present is predominantly geared towards young people. She is committed to producing accurate and engaging careers information for this readership, enabling them to make informed choices about their future careers.

Caroline is also the author of *Real Life Guide: Police Service* and *Real Life Guide: Childcare* and the co-author of *Real Life Guide: Care, Welfare & Community Work*, all published by Trotman Publishing.

Acknowledgements

Many thanks to the apprentices – Lee Barrass, Ed Wilson, Roxanne Moore, Robin Brisby, Jenny Jones and Charlie Grimmond – for agreeing to be interviewed and share their experiences, and to Sandra Dawson, Employer Engagement Support Officer at York College, for taking the time to organise the interviews.

Introduction

Looking at what you might want to do in the future in terms of education or work can be very daunting, with so many choices of courses and careers out there. You might be thinking that you don't want to stay in full-time education, but equally that you're not ready for work yet either. So what other options are there?

One you might be interested in is an apprenticeship combining both elements of work and education, enabling you to 'earn while you learn'. Using this book will help you better understand what an apprenticeship is, how they have developed, what is available and how to successfully apply for one.

You might be thinking that an apprenticeship is an old way of learning traditional trades such as carpentry or plumbing, so you may be surprised to find out that currently there are 190 different apprenticeships to choose from and more being developed for the future.

In this book, you can find out about the benefits of undertaking an apprenticeship as current apprentices view them (see Chapter 7) and also see how some famous names you may recognise have used their apprenticeships in their careers (see Chapter 8). Let's take a more detailed look at what is coming up in the book.

CHAPTER ONE: What is an apprenticeship?

In this chapter, you can find out about how apprenticeships have developed, what they offer, why they are popular, who they are good for and their benefits. It includes a brief history of apprenticeships, from the Middle Ages to the 20th century, before explaining more about the modern apprenticeship programme we know today and what the future holds for apprenticeships.

CHAPTER TWO: How an apprenticeship works

This chapter explains in detail how an apprenticeship works, including information on the structure of apprenticeship programmes, the different levels of apprenticeships available, what training they offer (including on the job and off the job training) and what you need to successfully complete an apprenticeship. You'll find out more about how you would be working, earning and learning on an apprenticeship.

CHAPTER THREE: Who offers apprenticeships?

So now you know what an apprenticeship is, but who offers them? This chapter gives information on the types of organisations that do and the wide range of industries they are available in. Sector by sector – from business, administration, finance and ICT to vehicles and transport – you can find out what kind of industry you could be working in and what kind of employer you could be working for. This chapter gives examples of some of the actual employers that are currently offering apprenticeships, from Orange to Rolls–Royce, British Gas to Kwik Fit, and McDonald's to Asda.

CHAPTER FOUR: How to choose your apprenticeship

This chapter answers some of the questions you may want to ask yourself if you're thinking about doing an apprenticeship, such as where you find out about opportunities, what sector and programme you might choose and whether an apprenticeship is the right thing for you. This chapter will give you the information to help make an informed decision about taking an apprenticeship in a sector suited to you.

CHAPTER FIVE: How to apply

In this chapter you can find out about applying for an apprenticeship, including information on the different application routes. You will also be able to get some tips on completing your application form and making sure it stands out from the crowd, what employers are looking for from you when you do apply and attending an interview.

CHAPTER SIX: Wales, Scotland and Northern Ireland

Apprenticeship programmes are available in Wales, Scotland and Northern Ireland as well as England, although they vary slightly from nation to nation. This chapter explains the differences in terms of what they are called and what types are available. If you live in Wales, you will have the same choices as people living in England, in terms of the types of apprenticeships available, and so the apprenticeships listed in Chapter 7 will be directly relevant to you. If you live in Scotland or Northern Ireland there are fewer types of apprenticeships available and some have different titles, although there are still plenty to choose from and many of them actually have the same titles. This chapter lists for you the apprenticeships that are currently available in Scotland and Northern Ireland. For those available in Wales, see the list in Chapter 7, but remember these will have a different name in Wales.

CHAPTER SEVEN: Directory of apprenticeships in England

Where Chapter 3 told you about the wide range of sectors that offer apprenticeships, this chapter looks at each of them in more detail. You can find out more about the career opportunities in each sector, what kind of person would be suited to working in each and the skills they might need, and which apprenticeships each of these sectors offers. In this chapter, you can read about job roles, work and training, entry requirements, salary once qualified and career progression opportunities. There are also case studies of apprentices currently working in some of the sectors.

CHAPTER EIGHT: After your apprenticeship

This chapter looks at what an apprenticeship can lead to, whether it is a full-time job, a better chance in the job market or higher-level qualifications that can help you advance your career. Get inspired by reading the profiles of some famous people such as David Beckham and Jamie Oliver who started out on an apprenticeship and went on to build highly successful careers.

CHAPTER NINE: Further information

If you're interested in finding out more, this chapter gives web addresses for organisations with further information about apprenticeships, including some that offer online vacancy-matching services and general careers information for all sectors covered in Chapter 7. This includes information on Sector Skills Councils, standard-setting bodies and which industries or sector and apprenticeships each one covers.

PART ONE

OPTIONS AND DECISIONS

CHAPTER ONE

What is an apprenticeship?

An apprenticeship is a system of training a new generation of practitioners in particular skills. Apprenticeships provide a structured programme of training with an employer. Apprentices learn on the job, earning a wage and gaining skills at the same time. They also work towards nationally recognised qualifications. Apprentices build their careers from an apprenticeship.

You may think apprenticeships are a modern invention. In fact, apprenticeships have been around in some form or other for hundreds of years. Originally they involved training in an art, craft or trade.

The Scottish engineer Thomas Telford, who was responsible for designing the Menai Bridge in North Wales (one of the first modern suspension bridges in the world), started out as apprentice in the mid-1700s to a stonemason before moving to London to work on extensions of Somerset House. The new town Telford was named in his honour.

A history of apprenticeships

Apprenticeships have a long tradition in the UK, dating back to around the 12th century and flourishing by the 14th century. Apprenticeships became prominent in medieval Europe with the emergence of Craft Guilds.

Jargon Buster: Craft Guilds

A Craft Guild was an association of craftsmen in a particular trade. They were formed when a group of craftsmen engaged in the same occupation joined together. There were Craft Guilds for every trade or craft performed in a medieval city or town, including, for example, carpenters, shoemakers and bakers.

During the Middle Ages, a Craft Guild apprentice was sent to work for a 'master' during his early teens. The master was charged with teaching a trade or craft. A legal agreement defined the relationship between master and apprentice, and the duration and conditions of their relationship.

The standard apprenticeship in the Middle Ages lasted between five and nine years, depending on the trade. During this time, the apprentice received board, lodgings and training, but no wages. Apprentices trained for roles such as carpenter, painter, clothmaker, baker, shoemaker and candlemaker. Most apprentices were males, but female apprentices were found in roles such as seamstress, tailor, baker and stationer.

Apprenticeships expanded in the following centuries, with new legislation on working conditions and environment. During the Industrial Revolution a new kind of apprenticeship developed, in which the employer was the factory owner and the apprentice, after a period of training, became a factory worker. In 1802, the Health and Morals of Apprentices Act was passed. This legislation prescribed a 12-hour working day and a requirement that factory apprentices were taught reading, writing and arithmetic.

By the late 19th century, apprenticeships had spread from trades such as building and printing to include the newer industries of engineering and shipbuilding, and later to plumbing and electrical work. During the 20th century, however, apprenticeships became less important. By the mid-1960s there was growing criticism of apprenticeship training, which was seen as being male-dominated and failing to embrace new and expanding occupations. Traditional apprenticeships reached their lowest point in the 1970s when training programmes were rare.

Apprenticeships reformed

Fast-forward to 1994 when the government introduced a new apprenticeship programme, based on frameworks that are now devised by Sector Skills Councils. Each apprenticeship has its own framework, which sets out in a document how the apprenticeship programme works and what you will need to achieve to complete it.

Jargon Buster: Sector Skills Councils   ❗

Sector Skills Councils are state-sponsored, employer-led organisations that were set up in 2002 to speak on behalf of employers on skills issues. They explain the needs of business to providers of education and training and are also responsible for designing apprenticeship frameworks.

Since the mid-1990s, governments have been investing in apprenticeships and reforming the apprenticeship programme. The result of these changes has led to significant improvement in the quality of apprenticeships.

Apprenticeships today

Each year, apprenticeships are begun and successfully completed by thousands of young people. In fact, more than 100,000 learners now leave the programme each year after completing all elements of the framework. By 2011, more than 900,000 learners will have completed a full apprenticeship. This just shows how popular apprenticeships are these days.

Today, apprenticeships are no longer only available in the perceived 'traditional' roles such as electrician, plumber or joiner. They have actually expanded into a huge range of sectors – from hospitality to health and social care, from financial services to retail. Apprenticeships today also combine on-the-job training with nationally recognised qualifications.

At present, apprenticeships are available to anyone over the age of 16. There are different entry requirements depending on the occupation: you can find out more about these and training/qualifications for a large number of apprenticeships in Chapter 7.

The future looks bright for apprenticeships as well. The coalition government announced in November 2010 that it would be spending £605 million on new apprenticeships with the aim of getting 75,000 new places for adults on schemes by 2014–15.

Why are apprenticeships popular?

As an apprentice, you will learn on the job, build up the knowledge and skills that employers want and gain valuable qualifications at the same time. Apprenticeships are a popular choice because the skills you develop will make you more employable and offer you greater prospects for future career progression.

An Apprenticeship also offers you the chance to earn while you learn. You will be doing real work for a real employer and, as an employee, you will be earning a wage and working alongside experienced staff to gain job-specific skills. You will also spend some time training off the job with a learning provider.

Jargon Buster: Learning Providers !

Learning providers are responsible for the training part of an apprenticeship that takes place off the job and is based in a classroom. A learning provider may be an independent training organisation or a college of further education.

Apprenticeships are becoming increasingly popular for employers too, as businesses throughout the country are realising the benefits that an apprenticeship can bring. Having apprentices and therefore, in time, a well-trained workforce, can help businesses to make money.

Who are apprenticeships good for?

If you're the kind of person who is keen to get out of the classroom and into the world of work then they offer a great opportunity to do so, especially if you enjoy learning through hands-on experience. You will be earning too, so you get the best of both worlds. If this appeals, and you have a good idea of where you want to go with your career, then an apprenticeship could be the ideal choice for you.

So, in summary, what are the benefits? You:

- earn a salary
- get paid holidays
- receive training
- learn job-specific skills
- gain a nationally recognised qualification
- make yourself more employable.

CHAPTER TWO

How an apprenticeship works

The structure of apprenticeships

Each apprenticeship involves a structured programme of training that leads to a nationally recognised qualification or qualifications. On many apprenticeships you will work both on the job towards a competence-based qualification (often referred to as work-based learning qualifications) and off the job towards a knowledge-based qualification (often referred to as technical certificates).

Competence-based, knowledge-based: what's the difference?

Competence-based qualifications prove you have gained the practical skills you need to perform the job. Knowledge-based qualifications prove you have gained the technical skills and understanding of the theoretical concepts relating to the role.

Each apprenticeship framework has been developed by employers through the Sector Skills Councils to suit their particular sector. As mentioned in Chapter 1, Sector Skills Councils are employer-led organisations responsible for designing apprenticeship frameworks. Because apprenticeships are devised with the help of employers, the structured programme teaches you the skills you need to do a job well.

There are 25 Sector Skills Councils in the UK, each representing a particular industry. If you'd like to know more about Sector Skills Councils, and the sectors and apprenticeships they represent, have a look at Chapter 9.

There are currently more than 190 frameworks available across a range of occupational areas – from animal care to business administration, engineering to construction, retail to design. So this means there are over 190 different apprenticeships to choose from!

Apprenticeship levels

Apprenticeships are available at different levels on the Qualifications and Credit Framework (QCF), allowing you to choose the level most suited to you.

Scotland has an equivalent framework called the SCQF (Scottish Credit and Qualifications Framework). More details on where Scottish apprenticeships fit in this framework can be found in Chapter 6. For more information about the SCQF itself, please visit www.scqf.org.uk.

Jargon Buster: The QCF

The Qualifications and Credit Framework (QCF) is a new system for recognising qualifications. It contains new vocational (or work-related) qualifications, available in England, Wales and Northern Ireland. The QCF groups qualifications together into a number of levels, from Level 1 (equivalent to GCSE grades D–G) to Level 8 (equivalent to a postgraduate qualification), that place different demands on you as a learner.

Described below are the apprenticeships and the levels at which they are available in England. There are similar apprenticeships available in Scotland, Wales and Northern Ireland, but these have slightly different names. For more detailed information on these, please see Chapter 6.

Apprenticeship levels in England

There are three levels of apprenticeships:

- Apprenticeship (at Level 2)
- Advanced Apprenticeship (at Level 3)
- Higher Apprenticeship (at Level 4).

Apprenticeship

An Apprenticeship is at Level 2 on the QCF, and is the equivalent to five GCSEs at grades A*–C.

On an Apprenticeship, you will need to achieve:

- either a competence-based qualification and a separate knowledge-based qualification at Level 2; or
- an integrated qualification at Level 2 that combines competence-based and knowledge-based elements, and functional skills (see box on p 9)
- qualifications in maths and English to at least Level 1 and, if information and communications technology (ICT) is relevant to the occupation, a functional skills qualification in ICT to at least Level 1.

Advanced Apprenticeship

An Advanced Apprenticeship is at Level 3 on the QCF, and is the equivalent of two A level passes.

On an Advanced Apprenticeship you will need to achieve:

- either a competence-based qualification at Level 3 and a separate knowledge-based qualification at Level 3; or
- an integrated qualification at Level 3 that combines competence- and knowledge-based elements, and
- functional skills qualifications in maths and English to at least Level 2 and, if ICT is relevant to the occupation, a functional skills qualification in it to at least Level 2.

Higher Apprenticeship

A Higher Apprenticeship is at Level 4 on the QCF, and is the equivalent of a Foundation degree.

On a Higher Apprenticeship, you will need to achieve:

- either a qualification at Level 4
- or a Foundation degree or equivalent level qualification
- and functional skills qualifications in maths and English to at least Level 2 and, if ICT is relevant to the occupation, a functional skills qualification in this to at least Level 2.

Higher Apprenticeships are currently only available in a very small number of frameworks. Apprenticeships and Advanced Apprenticeships are the most common levels.

Jargon Buster: Functional Skills

Functional Skills are practical skills in English, maths and ICT. They are a new set of qualifications, launched in September 2010, and are available for all learners aged 14 years old and above. Functional Skills are not just about knowledge in the three subject areas, they are also about knowing when and how to use this in everyday life, so learners can get the most out of work and education. They are replacing Key Skills.

Working, learning and earning

While you are on an apprenticeship, your employer pays you a salary and supports you as you're working. Most of the training is on the job and in the workplace. The rest of your training will come from a learning provider (although in some cases it could all be given by your employer). Your employer will be responsible for giving you an induction into the company and into your particular role. You will have a manager at work who is responsible for helping you throughout your training. As your skills develop many employers will increase your wages.

A new national minimum wage for apprentices came into force from 1 October 2010. This is £2.50 an hour, and applies to time spent working and time spent training as part of the apprenticeship. The wage applies to all apprentices under 19 years old and to apprentices aged 19 or over in the first year of their apprenticeship. In practice, many apprentices earn considerably more than this minimum wage.

On the job, you will learn a combination of skills and practical activities in the workplace. Your employer or learning provider will make sure that your training suits your personal requirements, offers the skills you need for the job and fulfils national standards. There will be checks to make sure your employer is supporting you and regular visits from an assessor or training co-ordinator who will also be there to help you throughout your training.

Off-the-job training usually takes place at a local college or specialist training organisation, often on a day-release basis (usually one day a week) or over a number of days in a block. The amount of time you spend in off-the-job training depends on your particular apprenticeship. It could vary from one day every other fortnight to two days a week.

On Apprenticeships, Advanced Apprenticeships and Higher Apprenticeships you will receive a minimum of 280 guided learning hours (that is, time spent in training) per year. At least 30 per cent of these guided learning hours must be received off the job. The total guided learning hours for each apprenticeship vary depending on the requirements of the sector, and may include flexible learning methods such as e-learning or distance learning as well as more traditional methods such as group teaching and assessments.

In some occupations, there will be additional work-related tests or certificates you need to gain to complete the framework. For example, with many jobs in the manufacturing, engineering, agriculture and construction sectors, you will need additional training in aspects of health and safety, particularly in relation to operating machinery or working safely.

Apprenticeships can take between one and four years to complete depending on the type of framework. They vary widely in content and size and there is no set time to complete one: you can work at your own pace. How long it takes you to complete will depend on your ability, your previous experience and skills, the sector and the level of your apprenticeship.

After your apprenticeship

After your apprenticeship, you could carry on working, maybe getting promoted, or go on to take higher qualifications such as an NVQ Level 4 or a Foundation degree. Career progression for apprentices is excellent, with many advancing to highly skilled jobs and going on to enjoy successful careers.

CHAPTER THREE

Who offers apprenticeships?

As mentioned in Chapter 1, apprenticeships are becoming increasingly popular with employers. Many leading businesses across the UK, including Asda, British Gas, Aviva, Vodafone, BMW and the AA, are taking advantage of the benefits of Apprenticeships to motivate and train their staff and improve their productivity and outcomes. At present, more than 130,000 employers offer apprenticeships in England alone.

Even in these times of economic uncertainty, many large, medium-sized and small companies are expanding their apprenticeship programmes. This is because businesses that invest in training are more likely to survive a downturn than those that don't. And it isn't just employers that are investing in apprenticeships: in May 2010, the coalition government announced £150 million to fund 50,000 new apprenticeship places.

As apprenticeships have expanded into new sectors such as ICT, health and public services, they are now available at a huge variety of organisations ranging across the private sector, the public sector, multinational businesses and small local companies. Let's take a look at the different kinds of employers that are offering them.

Business, administration, finance and ICT

As an apprentice in these sectors, you could be working for any type of business and any industry, from global corporations to large public sector employers and from small firms to non-profit-making organisations.

You could be working in administration, marketing or sales, customer services, in a contact centre or in an accounts department. In the financial services sector you could be working as an apprentice for a bank such as Lloyds TSB, a building society such as Nationwide or an insurance company like AXA. In ICT, you could be working for a small company or a large employer such as BT or Orange.

Construction and the built environment

As an apprentice in this sector, you could be working for a multimillion-pound company or a small local firm. You could be working for an international construction company such as Carillion or a major building contractor such as Balfour Beatty.

Alternatively, you could be working for a building services engineering business, an electrical contracting firm, a specialist refrigeration and air conditioning to heating and ventilation company or a plumbing business.

Creative industries

The UK's creative industries sector is made up of a wide range of sub-sectors, from advertising, publishing, film, TV and radio through to crafts, design and fashion. You could be working for a large media corporation or one of the many medium-sized or small businesses. There are also publicly funded employers such as theatre companies, museums and art galleries.

You could be working as a digital artwork apprentice for a printing firm, an apprentice typesetter for a publishing company or as an apprentice in an events team at your local authority. Alternatively, you could be working in the cultural or heritage sector, in community arts or in the film, photography or music industries.

Energy and utilities

The UK's energy and utilities sector is made up of the oil, gas and petroleum industries, as well as nuclear power, coal, renewable energies, waste management and water. Apprenticeships in this sector are available in the gas, electricity, water and nuclear industries.

As an apprentice in this sector you could be working for a combined gas and power company, a gas firm, an electricity generator, a water utility, a combined water and waste company or a specialist contractor. You could be working for a large employer such as British Gas, E.on, npower or the National Grid.

Engineering and manufacturing technologies

As an apprentice in manufacturing you could be working in a range of industries including food, furniture, glass, textiles, metals and printing.

As a manufacturing apprentice you may work for a local glass company, a printing firm, in the automotive glazing industry or for a ceramics or food manufacturer.

As an apprentice in the engineering sector you could be working for a diverse range of employers, from specialised engineering companies such as Forgemasters, which is an open-die forging company (this is the shaping of heated metal parts) to hi-tech manufacturing companies in the aerospace and computing industries. You could be working, for example, for large aerospace companies such as BAE Systems or Rolls–Royce.

Environmental and land-based industries

The environmental and land-based industries sector is made up of 17 different fields, from agricultural livestock and floristry to animal care and environmental conservation. As an apprentice, you could be working in a range of different settings, from farms and wildlife parks to floristry and horticulture.

You could be working in a veterinary surgery or hospital as an apprentice veterinary nurse, in a dog grooming shop as an apprentice dog groomer, for a landscaping firm as an apprentice landscape gardener or for a local stables as an apprentice groom, for instance.

Health, public services and care

Health, public services and care cover a diverse range of sectors. These include employers in health care, social care, education, housing, community work, youth work and security services. As an apprentice, you could be working for a large public organisation such as a local authority or the NHS, for a private company or for a non-profit making organisation.

You could be working as an apprentice nursery assistant for a private day nursery or a pre-school, in a private dental clinic as an apprentice dental nurse or for a charity as an apprentice youth worker. As an apprentice care assistant, you would be working for a care provider such as a residential care home.

Hospitality, leisure, travel and tourism

The hospitality, leisure, travel and tourism sector includes employers across a range of industries from travel and tourism to hospitality and catering. It also includes employers in the active leisure and learning sector, which covers sport and recreation and health and fitness.

As an apprentice, you could be working in a leisure centre for a leisure management company such as DC Leisure or in a high-street travel agency for a global leisure travel group such as Thomas Cook. You could be on a Sporting Excellence Apprenticeship at a professional sports club such as Sheffield Wednesday, or on a Cabin Crew Apprenticeship with Flybe.

In hospitality and catering, you might be working for an international hotel chain such as Hilton Worldwide, for a giant fast-food chain such as McDonald's or for a local contract catering company, a school or college canteen or a restaurant chain.

Retail and commercial enterprise

This sector includes employers in the retail sector and logistics industry, as well as those in service industries such as beauty, cleaning services, property services and mail services.

As an apprentice in this sector, you could be working in retail for a superstore such as Asda or the Co-op or in logistics for a wholesaler such as Smiths News. You could be working in a service industry for a hairdressing salon such as Toni & Guy (a UK-based chain with salons worldwide) or for a specialist postal service provider such as Royal Mail.

Vehicles and transport

Vehicles and transport includes employers in both the retail motor industry and the passenger transport sector.

As an apprentice in the retail motor industry, you could be working for a national chain or a local company. You could be working for a car, motorcycle or truck dealership, an independent garage, a vehicle breakdown or rental company or a fast-fit centre. Large employers offering apprenticeships in the motor industry include, for example, BMW (UK) Ltd, Honda, Jaguar, the RAC and Kwik Fit.

In passenger transport you could be working in industries ranging from bus and coach travel to aviation and rail transport. As an apprentice, you may be working, for example, in transport engineering for Network Rail or Stagecoach Bus, or for Servisair on an aviation Apprenticeship programme at an airport.

For more detailed information on the types of apprenticeships available in these different sectors, take a look at Chapter 7.

CHAPTER FOUR

How to choose your apprenticeship

By now, you will have gained some knowledge about what an apprenticeship is, how they work and who provides them. This chapter will provide you with the relevant information to help you make an informed decision about taking an apprenticeship in a sector suited to you.

Where do I find out about opportunities?

A good place to start is the National Apprenticeship Service website at www.apprenticeships.org.uk, which has up-to-date information on available opportunities. It has an apprenticeship vacancy-matching service, where you can search for vacancies in your area and apply for them online. It also has a search facility for learning providers.

However, some smaller businesses may just advertise apprenticeship opportunities locally, so you will need to make sure that you look for vacancies in your local newspaper, careers information centre and job centre.

You may find that some more specialised apprenticeships are advertised on specific websites for that industry. Engineering Connections, for example, at www.apprentices.co.uk, is an engineering apprenticeship recruitment site where you can search for engineering apprenticeship vacancies in your area and apply online.

Many employers, particularly large ones, advertise apprenticeship vacancies on their websites, so you will need to think about checking individual businesses as well. You can also search for apprenticeship vacancies at www.notgoingtouni.co.uk.

Which sector should I choose?

Choosing the right sector in which to take an Apprenticeship will be greatly influenced by your interests and aptitudes. For instance, you may have an interest in and particular

Choosing your sector

Take a look at the following questions to help you choose which sector may suit you.

Do you enjoy learning practical skills?
If you answered 'Yes', you may want to consider:

- engineering and manufacturing technologies
- environment and land-based industries
- health, public services and care.

Do you enjoy using ICT skills?
If you answered 'Yes', you may want to consider:

- business, administration, finance and ICT
- engineering and manufacturing technologies
- creative industries.

Do you enjoy working with people?
If you answered 'Yes', you might want to consider:

- health, public services and care
- hospitality, leisure, travel and tourism
- retail and commercial enterprise.

Are you interested in travel?
If you answered 'Yes', you might want to consider:

- hospitality, leisure, travel and tourism
- retail and commercial enterprise.

Do you like to be creative and use your initiative?
If you answered 'Yes', you might want to consider:

- business, administration, finance and ICT
- construction and the built environment
- creative industries.

Do you have an interest in maths or science subjects?
If you answered 'Yes', you might want to consider:

- energy and utilities
- engineering and manufacturing technologies
- vehicles and transport.

aptitude for ICT, which may lead you to look at the business, finance, administration and ICT sector or at a creative industry such as film and television or graphic design. However, ICT skills are used extensively across the majority of sectors, so think more widely about how yours may fit into other settings such as engineering and manufacturing technologies or construction and the built environment.

Top Tip ☑

Think about your skills and interests when considering which sector to choose. Don't forget that many of your skills and interests may be useful in more than one sector, so do look a bit more widely!

Apprenticeships can be taken in everything from accountancy to zookeeping, so make sure that you choose an area that not only interests you now but will maintain your interest for years to come. The beauty of an apprenticeship is that you will learn and develop new skills in both your work and learning environments, so don't be put off by looking at sectors that may offer you a new challenge.

Which programme should I choose?

As you will have seen from Chapter 2, there are three levels of apprenticeships. However, whichever level best suits you, it will involve a combination of on-the-job and off-the-job training and learning.

Therefore, you should consider your options carefully before making your decision. Look at how the programme is structured in terms of how many days you spend in your work setting and how many you spend with your learning provider. You may feel you are more suited to a day a week learning spend the rest of the time working. This is known as a day-release programme. Or you may feel that working and learning in specific blocks – for example three weeks at work, one week with your learning provider – is a better approach.

You will also have to bear in mind that your apprenticeship programme is organised by a partnership between employer and learning provider and built around achieving the best

---

Top Tip ☑

If you are unsure about how your interests and aptitudes may fit into a particular sector, then have a look at Chapter 7. Look at the introduction to each sector and compare your interests and aptitudes with those of each sector. This will help you choose which sector may suit you best.

outcomes for all involved. Therefore, you may prefer the idea of day release, but your chosen apprenticeship may have a programme of block-release training. In certain circumstances, there may be some chance of negotiating this but the key thing to remember is why you want to take your chosen apprenticeship in terms of your interests, skills and future opportunities.

Is an apprenticeship the right thing for me?

You have already looked at what opportunities are out there, which sectors to work in and what programme you may want to follow. But is an apprenticeship the right thing for you? You will have to decide by using the information available to you, and you can use this book as a guide. Have a look at the following questions to help you decide.

- Do you like working in a team?
- Are you good at problem solving?
- Do you enjoy learning new skills?
- Are you willing to learn skills to help you get a good job?
- Do you want to earn while you learn?
- Are you creative?
- Do you like practical tasks?

If the answer to most of the above questions is 'Yes', then the chances are an apprenticeship is the right thing for you!

While there are many benefits to an apprenticeship, as you will already have seen, you also have to bear in mind that you may not be suited to a specific programme. You may prefer a classroom-based learning environment and do not want the hands-on aspect. You may feel you are not ready for a work-based environment or you may want to keep your options open in terms of deciding your career path. If you are undecided, then maybe an apprenticeship is not the right thing for you at this time, but could be in the future. Talk to your careers advisor, friends and family about what you are thinking about your future. If you don't feel you are suited to an apprenticeship right now, then consider the other options that are available to you.

CHAPTER FIVE

How to apply

You should now have an understanding of what an apprenticeship is, what it involves, how to find out about opportunities and which sector you want to work in. The next step is applying for a suitable apprenticeship.

In this chapter, you will learn about the different routes in applying for an apprenticeship. You will also get some tips on completing your application form and making sure it stands out from the crowd, what employers are looking for from you when you do apply, and attending an interview.

Things to consider before applying

- Do you have the right entry requirements?
- Are you prepared to travel?
- What type of programme is being offered?
- Will there be opportunities for further training or employment?
- Where will my learning/training provider be based?
- Is this the right apprenticeship for me?

You will need to ask yourself these questions when you're thinking about applying for an apprenticeship to make sure you are applying for the most suitable vacancy. If you are unsure, seek guidance from your careers advisor or contact the employer for more information. This will prove to them that you are able to use your own initiative and may be a good way of introducing yourself!

As you have already read, an apprenticeship can be offered through large multinational companies or a small local business. Competition for an apprenticeship can be tough, so you will need to make sure that you stand out from the crowd and really promote yourself to your employer.

Now that you have decided an apprenticeship is the right thing for you, the next step is to find a vacancy and apply.

Applying for an apprenticeship

Generally, there are three ways in which you can apply:

1. apply for an apprenticeship with an employer
2. apply for an apprenticeship through a learning provider
3. if you are working already, ask your employer directly.

If you're applying for an Apprenticeship with an employer, then the first thing you need to do is to find out exactly what is available locally. Take a look at Chapter 4 if you want a recap on finding out about opportunities and where to look for vacancies. Most businesses offering Apprenticeships will have very good links with a learning provider, which means that you don't have to worry about sourcing your own learning provider as well.

Another option in applying for an Apprenticeship is to look at certain learning providers. You may want to look at the Sector Skills Council website for your chosen sector to find out more about this. The web addresses of all the different Councils are given in Chapter 9. If you choose this route then the learning provider will pass on your details to employers linked into their programme for you to complete your work-based training.

If you are already in work, you might be thinking that you could progress further in your career if you undertook additional training, gained new skills or completed a new qualification. You may be able to achieve this if your employer supports you in doing an Apprenticeship. In this situation, you will have to find the learning provider nearest to where you live or work and apply directly to them for a place on their programme.

Stand out from the crowd

As mentioned above, competition for an Apprenticeship can be very high so you will need to make sure that your initial application sets you apart from other applicants. Most applications are now completed online. However, you may need to phone an employer or learning provider to request an application form and then have to post them your completed form; you may be asked to send in a curriculum vitae (CV) as well. Whatever the procedure, the end result remains the same – you have to sell yourself to the employer or learning provider to make sure you are chosen for interview. You may already have certain qualifications of a high standard, but if you send in a poor application form then you will not get selected for interview.

Top Tip ✓

Here are some tips on how to complete your application form to make sure it stands out from the rest.

- Remember your application is your one chance to impress a potential employer or learning provider before attending an interview.
- You need to remember that the employer or learning provider knows nothing about you apart from the form in front of them. So you need to make sure that by the time the application form has been read, they will know more about you as a person, have more of an understanding about your skills and experience, and ultimately why you should be given the chance to attend for an interview and be successful.
- Don't forget, once you submit the form you can't change it – so make sure you stand out from the crowd!

You can apply for more than one vacancy at a time, so keep a copy of your application and you can adapt it for other vacancies you may be interested in.

Completing your application

- Make sure you read the vacancy very carefully! Be clear about what type of person is needed and think about how your personal qualities, as well as your skills, make you the person they are after.
- Give as much information about yourself as you can. Provide some examples of any hobbies or achievements that show you are the right person for the vacancy. Think about situations where you may have used particular skills that are relevant to the vacancy, and show how these can be transferred to your apprenticeship.
- Bear in mind that your potential employer or learning provider will soon work out if anything you have written about yourself is untrue, and you will get caught out.
- Make sure your spelling and grammar are correct. You want to give a good impression, so it is a good idea to carry out spelling and grammar checks before submitting your application.
- Check your application. It is a good idea to read through it several times before sending it in. Make sure you are happy with it and that it is a good reflection of yourself in terms of how you are as a person, your skills and qualities, and why you want the apprenticeship. If you are not sure then ask friends, family, teachers or your careers advisor for some feedback. You will also need to check that your personal details are accurate and appropriate. Make sure any contact numbers are correct and email addresses do not give the wrong impression about you!
- Take your time! You want to give the best possible impression to your potential employer or training provider, so think about your answers carefully. Think about writing out a rough draft of your application form before filling in the real one so you can make any changes or corrections. Once you submit your application, there will be no chance to add anything else.
- Send it in. Once you have completed your application make sure you send it to the right place! If you're completing it online, check to see whether it has been received by the employer or training provider. If you are posting it, make sure you address the envelope correctly.

So your application form has been submitted – but the work is not over yet!

Attending an interview

If your application has been successful, you will be asked by the employer or training provider to attend an interview. You have already grabbed their attention on paper, now is your chance to impress them face to face.

Interviews can be quite nerve-racking, especially if this is your first one, so have a look at the following advice, which may help you before, during and after your interview.

Before

- Be prepared. Find out more about the employer and the apprenticeship you are applying for. Think about some of the questions you may be asked, such as 'Why are you applying for this apprenticeship?' or 'What skills and qualities can you bring to this apprenticeship?'
- Read any information sent to you carefully.
- Confirm with the employer or training provider that you will attend your interview.
- Make sure you know when and where you are going and how you will get there. You will need to arrive in good time for your interview to help you relax and compose yourself. Arriving late will not give a good first impression!
- Reread your application and remember any examples of skills or experience you have given as you could be asked about these in more detail.
- Dress appropriately. You will want to make a good impression straight away, so the way you dress and how you present yourself are really important.

During

- Be polite. Whoever is interviewing you may want to shake hands initially, make sure you say something like 'Nice to meet you' and wait for the interviewer to ask you to sit down.
- Make sure you sit appropriately and maintain eye contact with the interviewer. If more than one person is interviewing you, make sure you look at all of them and do not just focus on one person.
- Listen to the question carefully and think about your answer before speaking. If at any time you want to hear the question again, then ask. This will not go against you and will tell the interviewer that you want to make sure you have covered everything they have asked you.
- Be enthusiastic. This is your chance to tell your employer or training provider why you want to do the apprenticeship. The interviewer will also want to make sure that they are offering the vacancy to someone who wants it, so be positive.
- At the end of the interview you may have chance to ask any of your own questions. Think about some questions relating to the apprenticeship itself or anything you are unsure about. Try to think about things such as future employment opportunities or any additional training rather than 'How much do I get paid?' or 'What holidays will I get?' While these may be important, it is likely you will have already had this information and may give the wrong impression about why you have come for the interview.
- Remember to thank the interviewer or panel for their time before you leave.

After

- Relax! Whether you are successful or not, you have done your best and gained some more experience.

- If you are unsuccessful, don't take this personally! Ask for feedback about your interview as this will help you next time around. Competition is strong but there are more opportunities out there so don't give up.
- If you are successful, then congratulations! Your employer or training provider will contact you about when your apprenticeship can start.

Top Tip

The main things to remember in the application and interview process are:

- find the right vacancy for you
- make sure your application stands out
- be honest
- be yourself
- don't give up if you are unsuccessful.

There are apprenticeship programmes to suit whatever you are looking for, and whatever employers and training providers are looking for from you. By using the information and advice above, you should be well on the way to hearing the words 'You're hired!'

CHAPTER SIX

Wales, Scotland and Northern Ireland

Apprenticeship programmes are available in Wales, Scotland and Northern Ireland. As with apprenticeships in England, they have all been developed by employers through the relevant UK Sector Skills Councils and are available at Level 2 and Level 3 of the QCF or Levels 4–6 of the SCQF to anyone over the age of 16.

Higher-level apprenticeships

In Wales, Higher Apprenticeships at Level 4 are available in a very small number of frameworks, as in England. In Scotland there are a very small number of Modern Apprenticeship frameworks available at Levels 8–11 of the SQCF. There are currently no apprenticeships available at Level 4 in Northern Ireland.

The focus of this chapter, therefore, is on the apprenticeship frameworks available at Level 2 and Level 3 of the QCF or Levels 4–6 of the SCQF.

The programmes all follow the same basic structure, offering people the chance of paid employment and the opportunity to gain nationally recognised qualifications through a structured training programme. However, they do vary slightly from nation to nation – in terms of what they are called, for example, and what types of apprenticeships are available.

How to find out about opportunities, where to look for apprenticeship vacancies and the application procedures are generally the same in Wales, Scotland or Northern Ireland as in England. Most of the advice, therefore, given in Chapter 4 and Chapter 5 is relevant to readers there. However, some websites are specific to Wales, Scotland or Northern Ireland with details about apprenticeship opportunities there; these are listed in the following sections.

Wales

In Wales, the levels of apprenticeships are:

- Foundation Modern Apprenticeship (at Level 2)
- Modern Apprenticeship (at Level 3).

Apprenticeship frameworks in Wales are generally the same as in England, but funded through the Welsh Assembly Government. This means that there are the same types of apprenticeships available as described in Chapter 7. However, Key Skills is to be replaced by Essential Skills Wales in 2011.

Careers Wales at www.careerswales.com offers general information on apprenticeships. It also offers an apprenticeship vacancy-matching service, where you can search for vacancies in your region and apply for them online.

Scotland

In Scotland, apprenticeships are at the following levels:

- Modern Apprenticeship (at Level 5 on the SCQF, the equivalent to Level 2 on the QCF)
- Modern Apprenticeship (at Level 6 on the SCQF, the equivalent to QCF Level 3).

In Scotland, there are over 80 different Modern Apprenticeship frameworks that contain the same three basic criteria:

- an SVQ (Scottish Vocational Qualification), NVQ or alternative competence-based qualification
- core skills (e.g. communication, problem solving and numeracy)
- industry-specific training.

MappIT at www.mappit.org.uk provides information about getting onto a Modern Apprenticeship in Scotland, a search facility for learning providers, and an online Modern Apprenticeship vacancy-matching service where you can search for vacancies in your area.

The Alliance of Sector Skills Councils Scotland website at www.alliancescotland.org also has information about Modern Apprenticeships, including information on the current frameworks available.

SCQF Level 5 Modern Apprenticeship

Modern Apprenticeships are currently available at Level 5 in the following areas.

- Agriculture
- Business and administration
- Construction (civil engineering and specialist sector)
- Creative
- Customer service
- Extractive and minerals processing
- Food manufacture
- Glass industry occupations
- Hairdressing and barbering
- Health and social care
- Horticulture
- Hospitality
- Land-based engineering
- Life sciences
- Providing financial services
- Retail
- Security systems
- Vehicle body and paint operations
- Vehicle fitting
- Vehicle maintenance and repair

SCQF Level 6 Modern Apprenticeship

Modern Apprenticeships are currently available at Level 6 in the following areas.

- Accounting
- Achieving excellence in sports performance (football)
- Active leisure and learning
- Advice and guidance
- Agriculture
- Apparel, footwear, textiles and associated businesses
- Aquaculture
- Audio-visual industries
- Aviation
- Beauty therapy
- Business and administration
- Children's care, learning and development
- Construction
- Construction (craft occupations)
- Construction (technical occupations)
- Contact centres
- Creative
- Customer service
- Dental nursing
- Driving goods vehicles
- Electricity industry
- Electrotechnical services
- Engineering
- Engineering construction
- Equine industry
- Extractive and minerals processing
- Food manufacture
- Gamekeeping and wildlife management
- Gas industry
- Glass industry
- Hairdressing and barbering
- Health and social care
- Heating, ventilation, air conditioning and refrigeration (HVACR)
- Horticulture
- Hospitality
- Housing management
- ICT professional
- ICT user
- Land-based engineering
- Learning and development
- Life sciences
- Management
- Nail services
- Occupational health and safety practice
- Oil and gas extraction
- Photo imaging
- Plumbing
- Polymer processing
- Providing financial services
- Rail transport engineering
- Retail
- Security systems
- Spa therapy
- Storage and warehousing
- Supervisors in vehicle-fitting operations
- Supply chain management
- Traffic office
- Transport engineering and maintenance
- Travel services
- Trees and timber
- Vehicle body and paint operations
- Vehicle maintenance and repair
- Water industries
- Wind turbine operation and maintenance
- Youth work

Northern Ireland

In Northern Ireland apprenticeships are at the following levels:

- Apprenticeship (at Level 2)
- Apprenticeship (at Level 3).

ApprenticeshipsNI is the Northern Ireland apprenticeship programme. There are over 100 different apprenticeship frameworks of the following standard format:

- a competence-based qualification (e.g. an NVQ)
- essential skills (e.g. communication and application of number)
- a knowledge-based qualification (e.g. a technical certificate)
- other mandatory or optional elements as specified by the particular industry.

You can find out more about apprenticeships in Northern Ireland on the Department for Employment and Learning website at www.delni.gov.uk/apprenticeshipsni, which gives general information, details of the current frameworks available and a search facility for learning providers (referred to in Northern Ireland as 'training suppliers'). It does not offer an apprenticeship vacancy-matching service but does advise those looking for an apprenticeship to contact their local jobs and benefits office/job centre/careers office, and has a search facility that allows you to find those in your area.

Level 2 Apprenticeship

Apprenticeships are currently available at Level 2 in the following areas.

- Accounting
- Active leisure and learning
- Advice and guidance support
- Agriculture
- Amenity horticulture
- Animal care
- Barbering
- Beauty therapy
- Contact centre operations
- Business and administration
- Communication technologies
- Construction
- Customer service
- Early years care and education
- Electricity distribution and transmission engineering
- Engineering
- Environmental conservation
- Equine industry
- Extractives and mineral processing
- Food manufacture
- Furniture production
- Glass industry
- Hairdressing
- Health and social care
- Hospitality and catering
- ICT services and development
- ICT user
- Laboratory technician (generic)
- Mechanical engineering service (HVACR)
- Mechanical engineering service (plumbing)
- Motor industry
- Nail services
- Passenger-carrying vehicle driving – bus and coach
- Pharmacy services
- Polymer processing and sign-making
- Printing industry
- Property services

- Providing financial services
- Retail
- Security systems
- Team-leading

Level 3 Apprenticeship

- Accounting
- Agriculture
- Amenity horticulture
- Animal care
- Barbering
- Beauty therapy
- Business and administration
- Children's care, learning and development
- Construction crafts
- Contact centre operation
- Customer service
- Electricity distribution and transmission engineering
- Electrotechnical services
- Engineering
- Environmental conservation
- Equine industry
- Extractives and minerals processing
- Floor covering
- Food manufacture
- Furniture production
- Glass industry occupations
- Hairdressing
- Health and social care
- Hospitality and catering
- Instructing physical activity and exercise
- IT services and development
- IT user
- Laboratory technician (generic)
- Land-based engineering

- Travel services
- Youth work
- Warehousing and storage

- Leisure operations and developments
- Logistics operations management
- Management
- Mechanical engineering service (HVACR)
- Mechanical engineering service (plumbing)
- Nail services
- Natural gas installation, maintenance and network operations
- Pharmacy services
- Playwork
- Polymer processing
- Print production
- Property services
- Providing financial services
- Rail transport engineering
- Retail
- Security systems
- Sign-making
- Stonemasonry
- Telecommunications
- Travel services
- Vehicle body and paint operations
- Vehicle fitting operations
- Vehicle maintenance and repair
- Vehicle parts operations
- Vehicle selling
- Water utility operations
- Youth work

PART TWO

DIRECTORY OF APPRENTICESHIPS

CHAPTER SEVEN

Directory of apprenticeships in England

In Chapter 3, you will have read about the wide range of industry sectors that offer apprenticeships. This chapter looks at each of these sectors in more detail. You can find out more about the career opportunities available in each, what kind of person would be suited to working in them and the skills they might need, and which apprenticeships are on offer. There is information on:

- job roles
- work and training
- entry requirements
- salary once qualified
- progression.

BUSINESS, ADMINISTRATION, FINANCE AND ICT

Together, these sectors cover a vast range of career opportunities essential for the smooth running of businesses and organisations throughout the UK. Business and administration is a huge sector, employing around 4.7 million people in administrative roles alone, as well as those in management roles from team leaders to supervisors and company directors and roles in sales, marketing, human resources and customer service. Organisations also need people to look after their finances and ICT systems, from accountants and payroll staff to website designers and ICT support.

As an apprentice in these sectors, you could be working for any type of business and in any industry, from global corporations to large public sector employers, from small firms to non-profit-making organisations. A wide range of career opportunities is available. As an apprentice you could be training, for example, to become an accounts clerk, customer service representative, personal assistant, financial advisor, insurance clerk, junior sales manager or an ICT professional, such as a software developer or system support technician.

The skills you need will vary depending on the role and sector you are working in. If you have a good head for figures and a business brain you may be interested in roles in finance and accountancy. If you have good communication and organisational skills you may be suited to a role in administration. If you can work logically and methodically and enjoy problem solving then working in an ICT role may be an option; if you are a good team player with an excellent telephone manner then a career in a customer services environment may interest you. Whichever sector you are working in, both ICT and communication skills will be important in many roles.

You may be interested in a position in these sectors if you:

- have an interest in the world of business and commerce
- enjoy communicating with a range of people
- like to be organised and show initiative
- have an interest in numeracy and ICT subjects
- enjoy responsibility and working in a team.

Depending on the role, it may also be useful to:

- enjoy maths and have a head for figures
- like persuading people or selling things
- have an interest in customer service
- have a passion for ICT
- enjoy leading a team.

Apprenticeships are available in the following sectors.

- Accounting
- Advising on financial products

- Business and administration
- Contact centres
- Customer service
- IT professionals
- IT and telecoms professionals
- IT user
- Marketing and communications
- Payroll
- Providing financial services
- Sales and telesales
- Team leading and management.

For information on the relevant Sector Skills Councils, which industries and apprenticeships they represent and important websites where you can find out more about apprenticeships and careers in this sector, refer to Chapter 9.

Accounting

This apprenticeship offers a route into careers in finance and accountancy. On this apprenticeship, you could be working for any type of business and in any industry, from large public sector organisations to global corporations, and from small firms to non-profit-making businesses.

There are currently around 1.57 million people working in accounting-related occupations in the UK.

Job roles

Level 2 (Apprenticeship) jobs comprise:

- accounts assistant
- accounts clerk
- cashier
- credit control clerk
- data input clerk
- finance assistant
- purchase ledger clerk
- sales ledger clerk.

Level 3 (Advanced Apprenticeship) roles are:

- accounts assistant
- assistant management accountant
- junior accounts
- finance assistant
- trainee accountant
- trainee accounting technician.

Work and training

This programme provides a structured approach to training and developing prospective accountants, who understand the needs of an organisation, its customers and the sector in which it operates.

Accountancy is a highly skilled profession with staff working at many different levels. Your job role will depend on your employer and the level of apprenticeship you are working at. On the Apprenticeship, you will work four days on the job and one day off the job towards a Level 2 Certificate in Accounting, and on the Advanced Apprenticeship towards a Level 3 Diploma in Accounting.

Roles include accounting for cash and credit transactions with job titles such as accounts clerk or finance assistant. You will be helping accountants to keep financial records and prepare accounts. On the Apprenticeship, you could be learning how to prepare financial documents and records, maintain the cash book and petty cash records and process ledger transactions. On the Advanced Apprenticeship, you may also learn about cash management, how to prepare accounts for sole traders and partnerships and complete tax returns.

Depending on whether you work for a large or small company, you could be specialising in one area, such as sales, or doing a wide range of tasks, as well as handling banking and petty cash.

Entry requirements

You will initially be assessed as to your suitability to complete the programme. For Apprenticeships, you will not need previous accounting experience, but you must like working with numbers and be able to show the potential for developing good communication skills. For Advanced Apprenticeships, you should normally have either completed an Apprenticeship in Accounting or have GCSE maths grade A*–C or equivalent, good communication skills and vocational experience.

It is also important that you are numerate and literate, can pay attention to detail and appreciate the importance of confidentiality in relation to accounting work. A good head for figures and a business brain would be useful.

Salary once qualified

You could earn between £12,000 and £16,000 depending on the role.

Progression

If you successfully complete the Apprenticeship, you can progress to the Advanced Apprenticeship and then the Higher Apprenticeship. On the Higher Apprenticeship, you work towards the Association of Accounting Technicians (AAT) Level 4 Diploma in Accounting.

If you complete the Higher Apprenticeship you can progress to professional accountancy qualifications. These can lead to membership of:

- the AAT
- Institute of Chartered Accountants in England and Wales
- Chartered Association of Certified Accountants
- Chartered Institute of Management Accountants
- Chartered Institute of Public Finance and Accountancy.

Progression can then take you into specialist roles such as internal or external auditor, credit controller, senior management accountant, tax specialist, business advisor or chief financial accountant.

Alternatively, following the Level 3 or 4 qualification, you may choose to enter a higher education course in a subject related to accounting, banking, insurance or other financial services.

Business and administration

On this apprenticeship, you will gain a solid foundation in business and administration. You will be working in an important support role in a business or organisation and be learning how to handle day-to-day tasks in an office and helping make sure things run smoothly.

Administration is essential to all businesses and organisations, whatever their product, function or sector. There are around 4.7 million people in the UK working in the field: business and administration is a vast sector.

Job roles

Level 2 (Apprenticeship) roles are:

- administration assistant
- clerical assistant
- data entry clerk
- filing/records clerk
- junior secretary
- office clerk
- junior legal secretary.

At Level 3 (Advanced Apprenticeship), there are the following jobs:

- administration clerk
- administration officer
- administration team leader
- database clerk
- executive officer
- office supervisor
- personal assistant (PA)

- secretary
- legal secretary
- senior legal secretary.

Work and training

On this Apprenticeship and Advanced Apprenticeship, you will work on the job towards an NVQ and off the job towards a relevant technical certificate. There are also pathways for legal administration and medical administration.

Qualifications at Level 2 are:

- Level 2 NVQ Certificate in Business and Administration and Level 2 Certificate in Principles of Business and Administration; or
- Level 2 Certificate for Legal Secretaries; or
- Level 2 Diploma in Medical Administration.

Qualifications at Level 3 are:

- Level 3 NVQ Diploma in Business and Administration and Level 3 Certificate in Principles of Business and Administration; or
- Level 3 Certificate for Legal Secretaries; or
- Level 3 Diploma for Medical Secretaries.

Your duties will depend on your employer and job role. As an administrator at Level 2, you will usually work under supervision and provide general administrative support to more senior members of the team. You will learn how to carry out a range of routine tasks, such as:

- making phone calls
- taking minutes in meetings
- typing up and photocopying documents
- sending the daily post and emails
- putting financial information together in spreadsheets.

You may learn spreadsheet, database and word processing software, as well as skills such as shorthand and touch typing.

As an administrator at Level 3, you will learn a wide range of more complex tasks. For example, you will find out how to:

- plan and organise events or meetings
- design and develop information systems
- manage budgets
- contribute to running projects
- deliver presentations.

You will work unsupervised, have a high degree of responsibility and may be supervising a team or office facility.

Entry requirements

There are no minimum entry requirements for the Apprenticeship and Advanced Apprenticeship since employers set their own criteria. You will, however, need to be numerate and literate and able to demonstrate that you have the ability to complete the programme.

It is useful if you can show a commitment to working in the sector, for example through work experience, and have some qualifications such as GCSEs, A levels or NVQs. It also helps if you can communicate effectively with a range of people, are methodical and have good organisational and time-management skills.

Salary once qualified

Your salary could be £12,000 to £18,000 depending on the industry and location in the UK.

Progression

There are clear progression routes from the Apprenticeship and it is possible, with extra skills and qualifications, to climb the business and administration ladder. As people progress in business and administration, they will take on extra responsibilities and manage people, projects and resources. Skills acquired in this role can also be transferred into other sectors such as event management, human resources or finance.

Successful completion of the Apprenticeship can lead to an Advanced Apprenticeship and more senior secretarial or administrative roles, such as a personal assistant, administration officer or office supervisor. With further experience and qualifications, there are good opportunities to move into higher-level management positions.

From the Advanced Apprenticeship, you could choose to take a higher-level qualification such as a Foundation Degree in Business Management, an NVQ Level 4 in Business and Administration or a professional qualification such as the Diploma in Administrative Management.

Customer service

Customer service is a hot topic – as more and more business is conducted online or over the phone, the quality of customer service plays an increasingly important part in the success of any business or organisation.

The demand for customer service exists in all sectors of industry and commerce and is relevant to many different job roles across many different sectors, from government to telecommunications. As a customer service apprentice, however, you are likely to be working in retail, financial services, call centres, hospitality or sport and recreation. It is estimated that at least three million people currently work in this area in the UK.

Case Study

Jenny Jones*

Jenny has just finished an Advanced Apprenticeship in Business Administration.

'I took A levels at school then went on to take a private management course in retail before becoming a store manager in a fashion shop. After working in retail for a while I decided I wanted to do something different so applied for a job as a personal assistant. I had a lot of customer service and administrative experience, which helped me get the job. I was a personal assistant to a manager in a large company, but there was no career progression in this post. When I saw the Advanced Apprenticeship advertised I realised it was something that would lead to somewhere else.

I was drawn to the Advanced Apprenticeship because the organisation I'm working for now is a big one with a lot of different departments, which offers scope for progression. It also appealed in that it led to a qualification. So there were two reasons for applying – the organisation and the qualification. During the programme, I took an NVQ Level 3 in Business and Administration and a technical certificate at Level 3.

Since I finished the programme, my employer has kept me on. My role is very broad, and involves writing letters, making phone calls and offering general administrative support to staff. I like the fact that I now have a Level 3 qualification, which means I can go on to higher education. I always wanted to go back into education at some point and getting this qualification has reinforced my decision.

I really enjoyed doing the Advanced Apprenticeship. It has also been very useful in getting me onto the career ladder, and you can't put a price on that. I didn't want to end up in just a basic administration role. I wanted something with further opportunities. And there are clear progression levels to a career in administration. I could go on to take a Foundation Degree in Business Administration (part-time while working), and then there are management qualifications too ...'

*Name has been changed.

Job roles

- customer service assistant
- customer service advisor
- customer service administrator
- customer service representative
- customer support agent
- customer support officer
- customer service team leader

- customer service supervisor
- customer service manager
- senior customer service advisor
- customer relations officer.

Work and training

As a customer service apprentice, you will usually work at the forefront of your employer's business, making sure that customers are dealt with in a positive, clear and pleasant way. Your main responsibility will be to make sure customers or clients get a high standard of service. You could be working in a variety of roles, such as meeting customers face to face, answering telephone queries, offering information and advice or handling complaints. To do this, you'll need to be able to absorb and interpret information, such as all the up-to-date details of your organisation's products and services.

On the Level 2 Apprenticeship, you will work on the job towards a Level 2 NVQ Certificate in Customer Service and off the job towards a Level 2 Certificate in Customer Service. You will develop customer service-specific skills and knowledge, including dealing with customers face to face and by telephone, dealing with customers in writing or using ICT, developing customer relationships and preparing to deliver good customer service. The programme will develop your communication, listening and problem-solving skills.

On the Advanced Apprenticeship, you will work on the job towards a Level 3 NVQ Diploma in Customer Service and off the job towards a Level 3 Certificate in Customer Service. The Advanced Apprenticeship relates to supervision of customer service and making improvements to benefit customers and the organisation. Your role as a junior manager or supervisor may involve leading a team, organising the promotion of products and services to customers, improving customer relations, solving problems, processing complaints and developing your own and others' customer service skills.

Entry requirements

There are no minimum entry requirements for the Apprenticeship programme except where employers set their own criteria. It may, however, be an advantage to have four GCSEs at grades A*–C, including English and maths. For the Advanced Apprenticeship, you may need a Level 2 customer service qualification.

You will have to be assessed and demonstrate your potential to complete the programme. It is important to have good communication skills, including an excellent telephone manner, be a good team player and have the ability to develop organisational skills. It helps if you are patient, polite and non-judgemental in character. You will also need to look presentable.

Salary once qualified

You could earn between £10,000 and £17,000 depending on your role.

Progression

After successfully completing the Apprenticeship, you can progress on to the Advanced Apprenticeship and then higher qualifications such as a relevant NVQ at Level 4 or a Foundation degree.

Strong customer service skills can lead to many different career opportunities. These may include promotion to team leader, supervisor, trainer and managerial roles. It may be possible to specialise in a particular sector, such as finance, or transfer your skills into a new area such as marketing or human resources.

IT user

ICT is sometimes known as just IT (information technology), as in the title of this apprenticeship.

On this apprenticeship, you will learn a wide range of general computing and ICT skills and you could be employed in a wide variety of industries. Having the ability to use ICT effectively means you will be able to work in the sector of your choice, from banking through retail to music production.

ICT user skills are important for people employed in all sectors, with around 77 per cent of the UK's workforce of 27 million using ICT as part of their day-to-day work. Those who spend a significant amount of time using a computer system rely on having the right ICT user skills and knowledge to perform their role effectively.

Job roles

Roles under this apprenticeship vary widely:

- ICT user support
- ICT helpdesk
- website designer
- administrator.

Work and training

You will work on the job towards an ITQ (the new ICT user NVQ) and off the job towards a technical certificate. These qualifications are at Level 2 for the Apprenticeship and Level 3 for the Advanced Apprenticeship. You will learn how to operate computers and databases and how to use and maintain IT systems and networks. You could be using a wide variety of applications, from design and desktop publishing software to data management or computerised accounting packages. On the Apprenticeship, you will be working under supervision; on the Advanced Apprenticeship you will take on more of a specialised role.

'ICT user' is not normally a job title but rather a specific set of skills that most employers need their employees to have. On this Apprenticeship, you will be learning skills that can be used to get the most out of the organisation's systems to benefit the business. Businesses use ICT for a wide range of functions, such as keeping track of finances, managing customer relationships and supporting the rapid processing of orders and enquiries and stock control.

On the Apprenticeship, you will develop the skills you need for your job. Roles vary widely and could include, for example, working in:

- the finance sector as an insurance administrator
- banking as a clerk
- an accounts department managing the wages
- the design and printing sector as a graphic designer
- newspapers and magazines in desktop publishing
- the creative arts as a music composer, music engineer, or dance choreographer
- retail and logistics as a stock controller
- the ICT industry as a website designer, in user support or on a helpdesk or as a trainer
- in education as a school administrator
- administration as a personal assistant.

At the end of the programme, you will have achieved the ICT skills you need, tailored to the sector of your choice. You will be familiar with ICT best practice as well as an organisation's business procedures and objectives.

Entry requirements

There is no standard entry requirement other than an interest in ICT and the ability and motivation to succeed and complete the programme. Employers, however, set their own criteria and may require you to have four or five GCSEs at grade C or above, including English, maths and possibly science for the Apprenticeship. For the Level 3 Advanced Apprenticeship, you may be expected to have the Level 2 Apprenticeship, A levels or the equivalent or work experience.

It is important that you are willing to communicate effectively with a range of people and enjoy being part of a team. It also helps if you enjoy solving problems, have organisational skills and can work logically and methodically.

Salary once qualified

You may earn from around £12,000 to £16,000 or more, depending on the role.

Progression

On successful completion of the Apprenticeship, you will be able to progress to an Advanced Apprenticeship and then to higher education, for example a Foundation degree followed by a full honours degree.

From the Advanced Apprenticeship, you can progress into management roles, particularly if the Apprenticeship framework is linked to a company's management development programme. The practical skills you gain on the job will be those suited to the organisation's business.

Providing financial services

This apprenticeship prepares you for a career in financial services. You will be helping customers make transactions – whether these relate to their bank account, loan, insurance policy, mortgage or credit card. On this apprenticeship, you would be working in the financial services sector, for example at a bank, building society or an insurance company.

The financial services sector is a big one that effectively controls the UK economy. The sector comprises a large number of financial businesses, from sole trader independents to global public limited companies. There are more than 34,000 financial services firms in the UK, operating more than 50,000 establishments and employing almost 1.2 million individuals.

Job roles

Roles covered by this apprenticeship are:

- insurance clerks in a number of areas such as financial services, claims processing, broking and underwriting
- customer service staff
- bank and building society counter clerks
- investment administrators
- pension administrators/advisors (at Level 3 only).

Work and training

On both the Apprenticeship and Advanced Apprenticeship, you will be working on the job towards an NVQ in Retail Financial Services (Level 2 or 3) and off the job towards a relevant technical certificate. The latter will depend on the role you are working in and the pathway you choose.

There are a number of pathways available at Level 2 and 3 including, for example:

- general insurance
- retail banking
- long-term insurance
- investment administration.

There is also a pension administration and a pensions advice pathway available at Level 3.

The general insurance route focuses on those who deal with, assess, investigate and settle insurance claims, as well as those working in broking and underwriting. You will learn, for example, how to handle and process new business, renewals and mid-term amendments, including the documentation. You may also provide administrative back-up in all types of insurance departments. The main tasks involve recording and checking information, dealing with clients and making financial calculations.

As a processing administrator, you would be transferring information from insurance proposal forms or oral instructions (e.g. over the telephone) into electronic systems and keeping computer records up to date. As an underwriting administrator, you would deal with insurance quotations. On the Advanced Apprenticeship you may be working in a supervisory role.

The retail banking route focuses on work in a bank or building society, call centre or remote financial services site. You will learn, for example, how to create and maintain customer accounts, handle payments and operate currency tills and counter services. You could be working as a cashier, operating cash tills and carrying out transactions, or as a customer advisor, setting up bank accounts for both new and existing customers. At Level 3, you could be working in a supervisory role managing other staff or be handling more complex accounts and business customers.

Entry requirements

You will initially be assessed on your suitability to complete the programme. There are no minimum entry requirements for the Apprenticeship, but you will be expected to be numerate and literate and should preferably have GCSEs (A*–C) in English and maths.

It helps if you can communicate with a range of people, show initiative, cope in busy conditions and are well organised.

Salary once qualified

Salary ranges between £12,000 and £16,000, depending on your role.

Progression

After completing the Apprenticeship programme, you may progress directly to the Advanced Apprenticeship in Providing Financial Services.

Progression routes are to supervisory, team leader or management positions. In insurance, it is also possible to go on to train as underwriters, claims officials, brokers or sales representatives.

For those who wish to continue the development of skills and qualifications beyond Level 3, opportunities exist to progress to higher-level professional qualifications, including:

- SII Diploma in Investment Operations
- CII Diploma and Advanced Diploma in Insurance
- Foundation Degree in Financial Services
- BA/MSc in Financial Services
- in-house training and development programmes.

CONSTRUCTION AND THE BUILT ENVIRONMENT

Construction and built environment is a huge sector, responsible for the work that goes into making or maintaining buildings, whether they're ancient castles or modern sustainable eco-homes. Construction is a multibillion-pound industry in the UK, employing over two million people and offering a huge range of career opportunities. Building services engineering is another important sector, employing over half a million people to supply our homes and businesses with essential services such as heating, electricity and running water.

As an apprentice in this sector you could be working for a multimillion-pound company or a small local firm. Within construction, you could train in a wide range of craft occupations including, for example, ceiling fixer, painter and decorator, bricklayer, stonemason, shopfitter or bench joiner, as well as technical roles such as civil engineering technician and plant mechanic. In building services engineering, you could train to become an electrician, plumber, heating installer, refrigeration and air conditioning engineer or a building services engineering technician.

The skills you need will depend on your role and the industry you're working in. If you enjoy physical and practical work you may choose one of many craft occupations in construction, such as those mentioned above. If you have a flair for organisation and planning you may be suited to a technical support role, helping to make sure projects run on time and to budget. If you have good practical and problem-solving skills and like to work with technology, you may be interested in a technical or engineering role in building services engineering. Creative skills are useful for some jobs, such as stonemasonry and joinery. For many jobs, you will also need a good level of physical fitness, and for some a good head for heights.

You may be interested in a role in this sector if you:

- like working in a team
- enjoy learning practical skills
- enjoy physical work
- enjoy problem solving
- have an interest in engineering and technology
- have an interest in maths, science and ICT subjects
- enjoy being creative
- are good at organising and planning.

Apprenticeships are available in the following sectors.

- Building services engineering
- Construction
- Electrical and electronic servicing
- Electrotechnical services
- Heating, ventilation, air conditioning and refrigeration
- Plumbing

- Set crafts
- Surveying

For information on the relevant Sector Skills Councils, which industries and apprenticeships they represent and important web addresses where you can find out more about apprenticeships and careers, refer to Chapter 9.

Building services engineering technicians

This Advanced Apprenticeship prepares you for a career in building services engineering. It covers the installation and maintenance of a range of systems and services in new and existing buildings.

Building services engineering is a vital part of our lives. Without it, there would be no heating, electricity or running water. The people working in building services engineering are the people who design, install and maintain the facilities that allow us to live and work in comfort and safety.

There are over 60,000 building services engineering businesses in the UK employing more than half a million people. As an apprentice you could be working for a multimillion-pound company or a small local organisation. And if you're interested in the environment, you'll get the opportunity to tackle the challenge of climate change head-on by implementing new energy-efficient technologies such as solar water heating and micro-wind turbines.

Job roles

Roles comprise:

- project manager
- installation and project designer
- estimator.

Work and training

On the Advanced Apprenticeship for Building Services Engineering Technicians, you'll develop technical and management skills in a variety of job roles, from design and installation and servicing to project management. On the job, you will work towards an NVQ at Level 3. Off the job, you will work towards the National Certificate in Building Services Technology at Level 3 at either a college or training centre.

This Advanced Apprenticeship covers the installation and maintenance of a range of systems and services in buildings on-site (for example, at petrol stations, quarries and processing plants) and domestic residences. This can include communication, heating and ventilation, lighting, air conditioning and refrigeration, water supply and plumbing, drainage and sanitation and electric power systems.

As an apprentice, you'll be working towards engineering technician status and be assisting engineers in their work. Depending on the actual job, you'll have a lot of contact with clients, design teams and professionals such as architects and structural engineers. Your work will vary according to your employer, but could include drafting designs on computers, estimating costs, supervising installation and maintenance and repair. You'll need to learn about and keep up to date with building regulations, safety guidance, technologies and new products.

Salary once qualified

After qualification, you could be earning between £20,000 and £23,000.

Entry requirements

To be employed as an apprentice, you'll need at least four or five GCSEs (A*–C) including English, maths and science or technology or the Higher Diploma in either Construction and the Built Environment or Engineering. Good communication skills are a must. It helps to have an interest in engineering and technology and an aptitude for design, and to enjoy problem solving.

Progression

If you successfully complete this Advanced Apprenticeship, you will have qualifications that can contribute to professional recognition as an Engineering Technician with the Chartered Institution of Building Services Engineers and the Institution of Engineering and Technology. You may choose to develop your career through further study towards Incorporated Engineer or Chartered Engineer status.

Bear in mind that building services engineering technician is a term that is used to describe a diverse range of jobs. There are therefore various career routes you could follow, including:

- design engineer
- commissioning engineer
- computer-aided design technician
- service and maintenance engineer
- estimator
- contract or project engineer
- contract or project manager
- quantity surveyor
- site supervisor.

Building services engineers usually progress by taking on more managerial responsibility. You might become a team leader, project manager, department manager or even a company director or partner. There are also lots of opportunities to work abroad.

Construction

Construction is a multibillion-pound industry in the UK, dealing with developing and building anything from a small housing estate to the 2012 Olympic stadium. It employs just over two million people and offers a huge range of career opportunities. This apprenticeship is therefore one of the broadest available and covers a wide range of occupations from bricklaying and painting and decorating to civil engineering and plant operations.

As an apprentice in this industry. you could be working for a very small building company or an international construction group. You could be working on sites in your region, throughout the UK or even abroad. And if you'd like to be your own boss, it's worth noting that more than a third of people in the construction industry run their own business.

Job roles

Jobs in the sector are:

- bricklayer
- built-up felt roofer
- bench joiner
- carpenter and joiner
- ceiling fixer
- civil engineering operative
- crane operative
- demolition operative
- dry liner
- floor layer
- general building operative
- lightning conductor engineer
- mastic asphalter
- painter and decorator

- partitioner
- plant mechanic
- plant operator
- plasterer
- roof slater and tiler
- roof sheeter and leader
- scaffolder
- shopfitter
- steeplejack
- stonemason
- technician (building, civil engineering and plant)
- wall and floor tiler
- wood machinist.

Work and training

The Construction Apprenticeship Scheme is a structured training programme, combining on-the-job training with off-the-job learning through day or block release at a college or learning provider. Apprenticeships are available at craft and technician level. You will work on the job towards a relevant NVQ at Level 2 for Apprenticeships or Level 3 for Advanced Apprenticeships. Off the job, you are likely to work towards the new Construction Diploma, which offers practical training and a broad technical knowledge of the building process. Construction Diplomas currently cover 29 of the most common construction trade qualifications at Levels 1 to 3.

Depending on your occupation, you may need to complete additional qualifications or training. For example, all bricklayers, stonemasons, roof slaters and tilers and steeplejacks need to achieve a certificate for abrasive wheels training. While all apprentices receive health and safety training, demolition operatives need extensive safety training.

If you choose to work in one of the interior occupations, you could be a ceiling fixer, fitting suspended ceilings in big modern buildings such as shops, offices and hospitals. Or you might work as a painter and decorator, which could, for example, involve applying heavy-duty coatings to bridges and steelwork or gold leaf to ornate fixtures in a stately home.

You may work in one of the trowel occupations, such as bricklaying or stonemasonry. As a bricklayer, you would use a variety of specialist tools to cut bricks and blocks to size and spread and join mortar. As a stonemason, you could be based in a workshop producing intricate stone carvings or work outdoors replacing worn elements on historic buildings.

You may instead choose one of the wood occupations. As a shopfitter your role would be to plan, build and finish the shop interior. Working as a bench joiner you would prepare and assemble doors, windows and staircases ready for installation. You would also create fitted furniture such as wardrobes and cupboards for buildings.

Plant occupations involve understanding and using heavy machinery, both on-site and in mechanical workshops. As a plant mechanic you would be looking after the machinery found on a construction site, including for example cranes, trucks, bulldozers and excavators. Your role would be to make sure these are running properly and repair them when necessary. As a plant operator, you get to use the machinery, possibly moving hundreds of tonnes of earth in a day or shifting some incredibly heavy loads.

Technicians provide support to other professionals working on particular projects. As a civil engineering technician, for example, your role may be to assist the civil engineer with project designs, prepare estimates for the amount and type of materials to be used and help to ensure that projects run on time and within budget.

Entry requirements

There are no set entry requirements for many of the occupations on the Construction Apprenticeship Scheme, although GCSEs in maths, English and technology may be useful for the calculations, measurements and theory. You will have to take an assessment to get onto the scheme.

Roles that are more technical tend to have specific entry requirements. For a plant mechanic apprenticeship, you will normally need four GCSEs (A*–C), including maths, technology and science. Candidates for a civil engineering apprenticeship normally need four GCSEs (A*–C), including maths, English and a science subject.

You will also need to be aged over 18 to train as a plant operative or demolition operative.

To work in a craft occupation, you will need practical manual skills to use tools and machinery as well as skills in communication, team work, problem solving and numeracy. As a technician you will need an ability in maths and ICT as well as negotiation and organisational skills. Creative skills are useful for some jobs, such as stonemasonry. Many roles will require a good head for heights and a high level of physical fitness.

Salary once qualified

Depending on your role, you could earn from £17,000 to £20,000.

Progression

There are plenty of training and development opportunities available in the industry, and with further qualifications and experience, craftspeople can move up the career ladder

Case Study

Lee Barrass

Lee is taking an Advanced Apprenticeship in Construction, following the stonemasonry route.

'When I was in my last year of GCSEs, I was looking for an apprenticeship in construction when a family friend, one of the best stonemasons in the country, suggested training in stonemasonry. I applied to the firm he works for and was offered an apprenticeship with them, which I was really chuffed about. I did well in my GCSEs and could have stayed on to do A levels, but I had my heart set on getting an apprenticeship and getting into work.

'Stonemasonry is a respected profession and a skill that not many people have. I really enjoy the work. It's incredibly hard to do when you first start, then you get the knack of it. The company I work for make coping stone, for example for the top of walls, and window-sills for new buildings. They also take on restoration work, such as replacing worn-down stone on church windows, so the work is varied. I could be out on site or in the workshop. The work can involve measuring, taking drawings and making templates, as well as the more physical work such as carving the stone.

'At the moment, I'm coming to college on one-week blocks; there are 13 such blocks throughout the year. I'm working towards the Advanced Construction Diploma and an NVQ at Level 3. I'd like to finish my apprenticeship and carry on working for the company I'm with now for a while. In the future, I'd like to set up my own business carving stone fireplaces or headstones, which involves letter cutting. I like the idea of doing decorative work and making nice things. In the longer term, however, I'd look to come out of stonemasonry work as it's very physically demanding. I'm interested in either building surveying or teaching as a career, and will look into taking higher education qualifications on a part-time basis.

'I'm glad I chose an apprenticeship. I didn't want to go to university and get into debt, and I think by leaving school and making money it helps you to value it more. I also think going straight into work helps you to mature, as you're mixing with older people.'

into technical and professional roles. Many jobs also offer a good grounding for progression into supervisory or management roles. There are also opportunities to become self-employed; self-employed workers progress by building their reputation and the size of their business.

Electrotechnical services

This Advanced Apprenticeship covers a variety of roles in the electrotechnical industry. Electrotechnical workers install, maintain and repair technology in a wide variety of buildings and systems. The industry plays a key role in other sectors such as construction and engineering. As an apprentice you would therefore be working on a wide range of projects, from wiring a new sports stadium to installing road lighting on a motorway.

With the increase in renewable energy technology, you could also be working on wind turbines or solar panel systems that turn the sun's energy into electricity, playing a key role in tackling climate change.

There are around 20,000 electrical contracting firms in the UK employing about 365,000 people. As an apprentice, you could be working for a small local electrical contractor or a large national company with several branches.

Job roles

Roles in the sector are as follows:

- electrical machine technician
- electrotechnical panel-beating technician
- highway systems electrician
- installation electrician
- instrumentation technician
- maintenance electrician.

Work and training

On this Advanced Apprenticeship, you will train on the job with an employer and off the job at a college or training centre. You will work towards a relevant NVQ at Level 3 or technical certificate at Level 3, depending on your job. You'll work as an electrotechnical operative, specialising in one of the six roles described above. Across all the occupations, you will learn how to work safely and in an environmentally-friendly way, and to identify and rectify faults.

As a trainee installation electrician, you'll be installing power systems, lighting, fire protection, security and structured cabling in different types of buildings, from homes and offices to shops and sports stadiums. Training to be a maintenance electrician would involve learning how to check these systems to ensure they keep on working effectively. For highway systems, you would be installing and maintaining street lighting and traffic management systems on roads and motorways.

Entry requirements

There are no set entry requirements for the Advanced Apprenticeship. It helps, however, to have GCSEs (A*–C) in communication subjects, maths and/or science or technical subjects, or a Higher Diploma in either Construction and the Built Environment or in Engineering.

Employers look for applicants who have an aptitude for technical subjects and an interest in technology. It is important that you have good practical and problem-solving skills and are able to follow technical drawings and other instructions. Good communication and mathematical skills are important too. You will also need a good head for heights, normal colour vision, a reasonable level of fitness and be willing to work in cramped conditions.

Salary once qualified

You could earn from £17,000 to £20,000 on qualification.

Progression

Once you're qualified to NVQ Level 3, you can progress to higher qualifications such as NVQ Level 4 or a degree, which will lead to further job opportunities at technician or management level. You could also progress into teaching or design consultancy work. There's also the opportunity to run your own business if you become self-employed.

Heating, ventilation, air conditioning and refrigeration

This apprenticeship covers a wide range of opportunities in the heating, ventilation, air conditioning and refrigeration (HVACR) industry. Heating and ventilation systems make sure we have fresh air and warmth when we're indoors whether in a shop, office, sports hall or cinema. Air conditioning and refrigeration systems ensure the air around us is not too hot or cold. People working in HVACR install and manage such systems.

As an apprentice, you could be working for a specialist refrigeration and air conditioning company or a specialist heating and ventilation company. There are also opportunities with local councils, supermarket chains and large building services companies. Working in this industry, you'll also be helping to protect the environment by installing systems that help customers reduce their energy consumption.

Job roles

Specific roles in this sector are:

- commissioning engineer
- control engineer
- domestic heating installer
- ductwork installer
- heating installer
- refrigeration and air conditioning engineer
- service and maintenance engineer.

Work and training

You will train on the job with an employer and off the job at a college or training centre. The NVQs and technical certificates you will work towards, at either Level 2 (Apprenticeship) or Level 3 (Advanced Apprenticeship), will depend on which area of the industry you are working in and your particular role. You may also have the option to work towards certificates relevant to your role, for example in fire safety, site safety or electrical safety.

In heating and ventilation, you could be working as a heating installer, fitting heating equipment and pipework in large buildings such as schools and office blocks. As a ductwork installer, you could be fitting ductwork and ventilation systems in large buildings such as shopping centres and airport terminals. As a commissioning engineer, your role would be to test systems to make sure that they do what the customer needs them to do. As a service and maintenance engineer, you would be carrying out regular maintenance and repairs on systems.

As an apprentice in the refrigeration and air conditioning sector, you could be helping to install, service and maintain refrigeration systems in buildings such as supermarkets and hospitals. Alternatively, you might be helping to install, service and maintain the systems that control air quality and temperature inside modern buildings. You'll be inspecting and testing equipment, spotting any faults and fixing them to ensure the systems work.

Entry requirements

There are no set requirements for apprenticeships and all applicants take an initial assessment test. It is recommended, however, that applicants with four GCSEs (A*–D) in maths, English, science and design and technology, or equivalent qualifications, will be best equipped to meet the minimum standard of the test. The Diploma in either Construction and the Built Environment or in Engineering may be relevant.

It is important that you have good practical and manual skills and are able to follow technical drawings and other instructions. Good written and verbal communication and problem-solving skills are also important. An interest in maths and science subjects and environmental matters would be an advantage. It also helps if you have a head for heights and are prepared to work in cramped conditions. You will also need normal colour vision and a reasonable level of fitness.

Salary once qualified

On qualification, you may be earning from £16,500 to £21,000.

Progression

Once you're qualified to NVQ Level 3, you can progress to higher qualifications such as an NVQ Level 4 or a degree, which will lead to job opportunities at technician or management level. You could also progress into teaching or design consultancy work.

Plumbing

Plumbing is a key part of the UK's construction sector and a continually developing industry. In recent years, environmental technologies have been integrated into the industry offering opportunities for plumbers to carry out a wide range of jobs. As a plumber, you'll not only be installing and maintaining central heating, hot and cold water systems and drainage; you'll also be helping to reduce our energy and water consumption by installing solar heating, rainwater harvesting or wastewater recycling systems in homes and other properties.

This apprenticeship covers training in a wide range of plumbing systems and their components. As an apprentice, you could be working on a diverse range of domestic, commercial or industrial projects, from installing a solar-powered hot water system and servicing boilers to laying underground drainage pipes. You could be working on a construction site or in a domestic setting.

There are around 20,000 plumbing businesses in the UK, with about 80 per cent of these being sole traders. The main employers are general building contractors that take on large contracts for office buildings, housing estates and public places, and there are also smaller companies that work for building contractors and private clients.

Job roles

There are two pathways in plumbing.

At Level 2 (Apprenticeship), you can train as a domestic plumber.

At Level 3 (Advanced Apprenticeship), the following roles are available:

- domestic plumber
- industrial and commercial plumber.

Work and training

You will train on the job with an employer and off the job at a college or training centre. On the Apprenticeship, you will work towards an NVQ at Level 2 and a Certificate in Plumbing at Level 2. As an apprentice domestic plumber, you will learn how to install basic cold water, hot water, sanitation, rainwater and wet central heating systems, as well as sheet lead weathering systems. You will use a variety of hand and power tools to cut, bend, join and fix materials such as copper and plastic. You will learn how to work safely and in an environmentally-friendly way, and also how to identify and rectify faults. You may also have the option to work towards relevant certificates, for example in fire safety, site safety or electrical safety.

On the Advanced Apprenticeship as a domestic plumber, you will learn how to install more complex systems as well as domestic fuel-burning appliances such as gas, oil or solid fuel boilers. As an industrial and commercial plumber, you will install heating, fuel supplies, specialist appliances and fire protection systems in industrial and commercial buildings such as factories, hospitals and shopping centres. You will work towards a relevant technical certificate and NVQ at Level 3 and then be able to enter the profession at a higher level.

Entry requirements

There are no set requirements for apprenticeships and all applicants take an initial assessment test. It is recommended, however, that applicants with four GCSEs (A*–D) in maths, English, science and design and technology or equivalent qualifications will be best equipped to meet the minimum standard for the test.

It is important that you have good practical and manual skills and are able to follow technical drawings and other instructions. Good written and verbal communication and problem-solving skills are also important. An understanding of maths and science is vital. It will benefit you if you have a head for heights as well and are willing to work in cramped conditions. You will also need normal colour vision and a reasonable level of fitness.

Salary once qualified

Pay on qualification varies from £17,000 to £21,000.

Progression

Once you're qualified to NVQ Level 3 you can progress to higher qualifications such as an NVQ Level 4 or a degree, which will lead to job opportunities at technician or management level. You could also progress into teaching or design consultancy work. Additionally, if you become self-employed you will have an opportunity to run your own business.

CREATIVE INDUSTRIES

The UK's creative industries sector is made up of a wide range of sub-sectors, from advertising, publishing and photo imaging through to animation, interactive media, film, TV and radio, computer games, crafts, design and fashion. Creative employment provides around two million jobs, both in the sector itself and in creative roles elsewhere. The UK is a world leader in culture and media, and the UK's creative industries are among the world's best.

In this sector, you could be working for a large media business or one of the many medium-sized or small businesses. There are also publicly funded employers such as theatre companies, museums and art galleries.

A wide range of career opportunities is available. As an apprentice, you could be training, for example, to become a junior interior designer or graphic designer, photographer, art gallery assistant or animation assistant. Alternatively, you could be working towards becoming a production runner, an editing assistant or camera crew assistant in film and TV, as well as a wide range of other creative roles.

The skills you need will vary depending on the role and sector you are working in. Imagination and a flair for creativity may be important for many of the jobs, but other skills are important too. If you are technically minded, for example, you may be interested in roles such as operating sound and lighting in a theatre. If you're good with your hands, you may like to work with the machines that manufacture clothes. In other roles, such as live events promotion or in community arts, you will need administration, organisational and people skills. In many roles, ICT skills are also essential.

You may be interested in a role in this sector if you:

- enjoy subjects such as art and design or film and photography
- enjoy using your imagination and being creative
- have an interest in culture and media
- enjoy working in a team
- like using ICT skills.

Depending on the role, you may also be interested if you:

- like organising people or things
- enjoy learning practical skills
- like technical subjects.

Apprenticeships are available in this sector in the following fields.

- Creative
- Creative and digital media
- Design

- Fashion and textiles
- Photo imaging for staff photographers

For information on the relevant Sector Skills Councils, which industries and apprenticeships they represent and web addresses where you can find out more about apprenticeships and careers in this sector, refer to Chapter 9.

Creative

The Creative Apprenticeship offers a range of oportunities in the creative and cultural sectors. As an apprentice, you could be working in a wide range of roles and sectors, from promoting live events in the music industry to operating sound and lighting in a theatre; from developing arts projects in the community to organising exhibitions in a gallery.

The Creative Apprenticeship programme was developed together by industry and Creative and Cultural Skills, the Sector Skills Council for the creative and cultural industries, which covers craft, cultural heritage, design, literature, music, performing arts and visual arts. The programme aims to meet the needs of these industries, which are dominated by a culture of unpaid work experience, by breaking the vicious circle of 'no experience equals no job.'

Job roles

Job roles have been broken down into the pathways listed below.

Community arts and development

- Arts/development officer/co-ordinator
- Community artist
- Contracts assistant
- Education assistant
- Fund-raising assistant
- Outreach worker
- Project co-ordinator/manager
- Youth worker

Costume and wardrobe

- Attendant/gallery staff/warden
- Costume designer
- Cultural and heritage venue operations
- Front of house staff, administrator
- Guide demonstrator
- Pattern cutter
- Repairs and alterations staff
- Sales staff
- School liaison officer
- Wardrobe assistant

Music business

- Administrator of live events
- Artist management
- Artists and repertoire staff
- Booking agent
- Marketing and communications staff
- Producer's assistant – live events
- Programmers and assistant
- Publicity and promotion staff
- Publishing staff

Music – live events and promotion

- Artist management
- Assistant stage manager
- Director's assistant
- Licensing/contracts staff
- Performer
- Production assistant
- Props assistant
- Technical assistant
- Wardrobe assistant

Technical theatre

- Lighting/stage electrics staff
- Production assistant
- Rigger
- Sound engineer
- Special effects and pyrotechnics staff
- Stage assistant
- Technical assistant

Work and training

The Creative Apprenticeship is available at Level 2 (Apprenticeship) and Level 3 (Advanced Apprenticeship) and consists of a vocational qualification at Level 2 or 3 and a theory-based qualification at Level 2 or 3. A Level 2 Apprenticeship is aimed at those entering the workforce. Through the structured training, apprentices develop skills and knowledge to work in a junior position for an organisation.

An Advanced Apprenticeship is more suited to people with previous work experience looking for a step up the career ladder. In some cases, you may, as a Level 3 apprentice, be performing managerial or supervisory duties in your role.

As an apprentice at both Level 2 and Level 3 you can choose from one of the following career pathways:

- community arts and education
- costume and wardrobe
- cultural and heritage venue operations
- music business (recording industry)
- music – live events and promotion
- technical theatre (rigging, lighting and sound).

Within community arts and education, you might be involved in developing community arts projects, including applying for funding and building partnerships with relevant local organisations. This role may involve managerial elements. As a costume and wardrobe apprentice, you could be sourcing, making and altering costumes. On the cultural venues and operations pathway, you might be working for a local museum or art gallery, dealing with customers, organising events and exhibitions and doing administrative work.

On the music business pathway you could be working for a record label, producing contracts, preparing royalty statements, working with artists and supporting marketing campaigns.

In live events and promotion, you would learn how to plan, promote and stage live events. This would involve, for example, booking venues and organising technical support and supporting artists.

If you choose the technical theatre pathway, you could be setting up and operating sound and lighting equipment and running and crewing an ongoing production.

Entry requirements

There are no set entry requirements for the Creative Apprenticeship. It is important to have an interest in the creative and cultural industries and a motivation to suceed. You will need to have the potential to complete the qualifications. It will help if you are able to develop your organisational skills and cope in busy conditions, as well as having good communication skills.

Salary once qualified

You could earn between £12,000 and £16,000 depending on your role.

Progression

Promotion may involve working on more important projects or progressing into management positions. Many people in these sectors are self-employed and progress by building their business and reputation.

On completion of the Advanced Apprenticeship, you could choose to move on to higher-level qualifications, for example a Foundation or Honours degree in a relevant subject, or take NVQs in management. Alternatively, you could develop your career through in-house development programmes.

Creative and digital media

This Advanced Apprenticeship covers a wide range of opportunities across the creative media industries, including TV, radio, film, digital graphics and photo imaging. As an apprentice, you could be working as a runner in a post production house or an assistant at a TV or film production company or web design agency.

The creative media industries are dynamic, rapidly evolving and converging. Employers look for committed individuals who have a good understanding of what it takes to work their way up in creative media – including the capacity to work hard, efficiently and in teams.

There are many possible roles, ranging from production and editing to camerawork, interactive media and photography. Many roles require a combination of technical and creative abilities.

Job roles

The following job roles are available in the sector:

- animation assistant
- assistant to the camera crew
- archive assistant
- broadcasting assistant
- editing assistant
- junior designer
- photographer
- post-production runner
- production assistant
- production runner
- production secretary
- technical assistant
- researcher
- web co-ordinator.

Work and training

This Advanced Apprenticeship is a new qualification designed to give apprentices know-how and experience and access to key industry contacts. You will receive training to prepare you for work in the creative media industries and take digital and creative modules pertaining to your job. You will receive on-the-job and off-the-job training and work towards nationally recognised qualifications at Level 3, including a relevant NVQ as well as the Level 3 Diploma in Media Techniques.

You will be able to tailor your programme depending on your focus, employer and job role. You may be able to select a combination of options, including:

- design for the moving image
- editing for sound and video

- photo imaging
- radio production, writing, editing and presentation
- production
- interactive media
- broadcast journalism
- camera work.

Your role will depend on your employer and which sector you are working in. You could be working in film or TV production as a production runner, doing all kinds of tasks to help everything run smoothly. Typically, your work may involve fetching and delivering items such as tapes and scripts, transporting crews between locations, making teas, coffees and lunches, and general administrative work.

Alternatively, you could be working as an assistant to a camera crew loading the film and providing general camera support. Camera crews work with extremely delicate, expensive equipment and are among the most highly skilled practitioners in any film crew.

As an apprentice working in photo imaging, you could be taking pictures in a variety of contexts, such as portrait or still life or on shoots for particular material. You would learn how to plan, organise and carry out photographic assignments. Your work may involve choosing locations, setting up lighting, selecting appropriate cameras, lenses and film and composing pictures, then manipulating the images you create using software packages.

Entry requirements

There are no set entry requirements for this programme. You will need to have good numeracy and literacy skills and strong ICT skills. It is important to have a real passion for digital and creative media and strong communication skills. You will also need to be able to think creatively and work well under pressure.

Salary once qualified

You may earn between £13,000 and £17,000, depending on the role.

Progression

The creative media industries are always changing; therefore it is important to keep up to date with industry trends and developments in technology through specialist training. With experience, there are good opportunities to move into management roles. Many people in these industries work as freelancers and may need to develop their marketing and networking skills to seek out new opportunities and build on their reputation.

On completion of this Advanced Apprenticeship, you could choose to move on to higher-level qualifications, for example a Foundation degree or Honours degree in a relevant subject.

Design

This apprenticeship covers all the areas from graphics to product design. As an apprentice, you could be working in a range of industries, including media, manufacturing, fashion and furniture. You could work for a design firm or a business that employs designers in parts of its operations, such as a textile manufacturer. While each industry requires specific skills, all designers work to come up with a concept that both serves a purpose and looks good.

In the UK, around 180,000 people are employed in design. If you'd like to be your own boss it's useful to know that around a third of designers are self-employed.

Job roles

Job roles in the sector are:

- furniture designer
- graphic designer
- interior designer
- product designer.

Work and training

The nature of your apprenticeship will depend on your employer. You could be working in graphic design, dealing with words and images to communicate ideas and information, or in product design, designing anything from vacuum cleaners to toys or furniture. Working in interior design, you could be designing commercial and domestic interiors, for example offices, hotels, shops and homes.

On the Apprenticeship at Level 2, you will learn all design team operations. The Apprenticeship covers everything from graphics to multimedia. You will work on the job towards a Level 2 NVQ in Design Support and off the job at college towards a BTEC First Certificate in Art and Design. You will be supporting designers in their role and will learn how to:

- research information and ideas
- develop and communicate design ideas
- develop design responses to meet agreed requirements
- contribute to producing detailed design work.

On the Advanced Apprenticeship, you will work on the job towards a Level 3 NVQ in Design and off the job towards a relevant technical certificate at Level 3. You will take on more responsibility for planning and managing your work and learn how to:

- clarify briefs and research information
- develop design ideas using materials, processes and technologies
- develop and present suitable design responses
- produce and present detailed design proposals.

In all areas you will be working from a brief, preparing visuals and agreeing the final design. You will need to work within the budget and to meet the deadline.

Entry requirements

There are no set entry requirements for this apprenticeship. Employers determine their own criteria, and some may ask for GCSEs (A*–C) in English and maths.

It is important to be creative and have a good eye for shape and colour. It also helps if you have good communication skills and can explain your ideas clearly. Computer skills will also be an advantage.

Salary once qualified

After qualifying, you could earn from £11,000 to £18,000 depending on the role.

Progression

On completion of the Advanced Apprenticeship, you'll be qualified to work as a design technician, design assistant or junior designer and be able to progress to higher-level qualifications such as an NVQ Level 4 in design management or a relevant Foundation degree.

Junior designers can progress to a senior position. With further experience they may take on team management responsibilities. Many designers move into self-employment.

Fashion and textiles

This sector covers the fashion and textiles supply chain, including the processing of raw materials, product manufacture, wholesale and trading activities and the after-sales servicing of products.

As an apprentice, you will be working in one of the sector's five main industries: apparel, footwear, leather goods, saddlery or textiles. There is a wide range of roles available, from sewing machinist, tailor and textile technician to saddler, leather goods designer and shoe repairer.

The UK fashion and textiles sector employs more than 340,000 people across around 79,000 enterprises. If you like the idea of being self-employed then it's worth knowing that small businesses and sole traders dominate the sector.

Job roles

Job roles are broken down into the following five pathways.

Apparel

At Level 2 (Apprenticeship), you could be a:

- dyeing and printing operative
- hand presser
- pattern cutter or grader

- sewing machinist
- tape sealing operative.

At Level 3 (Advanced Apprenticeship), roles comprise:

- garment technologist
- handcraft garment maker
- pattern or grading technologist
- quality controller
- sample machinist
- trainee and apprentice tailor/dressmaker.

Footwear

Roles at Level 2 (Apprenticeship) are:

- clicker, cutter, closer/stitcher
- customer-facing roles
- finisher
- laster, maker and welter
- quality inspector
- shoe room roles.

At Level 3 (Advanced Apprenticeship), you could be a:

- footwear repairer
- footwear technician
- orthopaedic/bespoke footwear technician
- supervisor
- technician.

Leather goods

Level 2 (Apprenticeship) positions are:

- customer-facing roles
- finisher
- leather processor
- quality inspector
- tanner.

At Level 3 (Advanced Apprenticeship), you could be a:

- leather goods designer
- supervisor
- technician.

Saddlery

At Level 2 (Apprenticeship), you could be a:

- craftsperson
- production operative

- retail/service operative
- trainee saddler.

Level 3 (Advanced Apprenticeship) positions are:

- production/quality controller
- saddler
- specialist craftsperson
- supervisor/leader
- technician.

Textiles

At Level 2 (Apprenticeship), you might be a:

- packer
- quality inspector
- textile machinery operative
- textile tester.

On a Level 3 (Advanced Apprenticeship) programme, roles are:

- coating and laminating machine technician
- fabric inspector
- printing machine technician
- technicians (dyeing, tufting and textiles)
- weaver (fabric and carpet).

Work and training

On the Fashion and Textiles Apprenticeship, you will learn the craft skills and technical knowledge that the sector needs to compete effectively. You will also take specific health and safety training. You will choose one of the five pathways outlined above.

On the Apprenticeship, you will be supervised and work on the job towards a vocational qualification at Level 2 and off the job towards a technical certificate at Level 2. On the Advanced Apprenticeship, you will take on more of a supervisory or technical role. You will work on the job towards a vocational qualification at Level 3 and off the job towards a technical certificate at Level 3. The nature of your work will depend on the pathway you choose.

As a pattern grader in clothing manufacturing, for instance, you would take a pattern and produce scaled-up and scaled-down versions to enable manufacturers to reproduce the same item in different sizes. As a garment technologist you would work with the pattern graders to oversee the sizing, fitting and testing of the pre-production garments. As a sample machinist, you would use a sewing machine to create the first sample of a garment design.

As an operative in footwear manufacturing, you would use a range of handcraft tools and semi-automated equipment to create footwear products from fashion shoes to trainers. You could be involved in each stage of the production process, from cutting leather to stitching the pattern pieces together and fitting soles and heels to the finished product. As a weaver in the textiles industry, you would be using highly technical weaving looms to create fabrics.

Entry requirements

There are no set entry requirements for an apprenticeship. However, you will need to be able to study at Level 2 or Level 3, as appropriate.

For many roles, practical skills and the ability to follow instructions, meet deadlines and work well in a team are important. Good ICT and numeracy skills are important for technical roles. Having an interest in fashion and textiles would be desirable as well.

Salary once qualified

You could earn between £11,000 and £15,000 depending on your role.

Progression

On successful completion of the Apprenticeship, you can progress to the Advanced Apprenticeship and then on to higher education, including relevant Foundation degrees or Honours degrees.

There are opportunities for operatives to progress into supervisory roles or higher-level roles such as technologist or quality control inspector. Technologists may move into more senior roles such as technical manager. It may also be possible to take a sideways move into a career in design or buying. There are good opportunities for self-employment.

Photo imaging for staff photographers

On this Advanced Apprenticeship, you will gain the skills and knowledge to become a staff photographer. As an apprentice staff photographer you could be working for a large commercial organisation, a government body, a university, museum or research institute or a host of other agencies formerly part of central government. The police service and armed forces also employ photographers.

Staff photographers also work in the medical sector and for publishers, and may be involved in scientific and technical work, fine art or architectural photography.

The photo imaging sector is made up of industries ranging from photography and picture imaging to large manufacturers and suppliers of photographic equipment, with over 8,000 photo imaging companies in the UK, and an estimated 8,342 small businesses. Photographers currently account for around three-quarters of the industry.

Job role

The single job role in this sector is staff photographer.

Work and training

You will work on the job towards the NVQ Level 3 in Photography and Photo Imaging and off the job at college towards the Level 3 Certificate in Image Capture.

The photo imaging sector has recently undergone the biggest revolution since the invention of colour photography – digital imaging. Photographers today can do everything digitally, from taking a picture all the way through to processing and archiving it. As an apprentice, you will learn how to carry out a wide range of tasks from maintaining photographic equipment to colour management and print processing.

You will also learn the following:

- studio lighting techniques
- studio technical photography
- in-situ lighting techniques
- in-situ technical photography
- additional lighting techniques
- additional camera techniques
- close-up technical photography
- copying techniques
- copying lighting.

You might also learn how to agree a photo imaging brief, choose and prepare locations, check image quality, process and print images and retouch photos using Photoshop.

Entry requirements

Minimum entry requirements are usually GCSEs (A*–C) in English and maths or equivalent, or a Level 2 NVQ in Photo Imaging. You will also need to be physically fit enough to carry heavy camera and lighting equipment.

To work as a photographer you need a variety of qualities and skills including:

- good eyesight
- close attention to detail
- good communication skills
- a creative eye for colour, shape, pattern, form and tone
- technical aptitude
- excellent interpersonal skills
- the patience to get the right shot even under stressful circumstances.

Salary once qualified

You could earn £12,000 upwards after qualification.

Progression

After completion of this Advanced Apprenticeship, you could progress to higher-level qualifications such as NVQ Level 4 in Photography and Photo Imaging or a Foundation degree in Photo Imaging.

Promotion may take the form of management, commissioning or editorial roles. Alternatively, with experience, staff photographers may choose to become freelance and set up their own business.

ENERGY AND UTILITIES

The UK's energy and utilities sector is made up of oil, gas and petroleum and also nuclear power, coal, renewable energies, waste management and water industries. Apprenticeships in this sector are available in the gas, electricity, water and nuclear industries. The gas industry is responsible for the transmission, distribution and supply of domestic gas, the electricity industry keeps power flowing into our homes and the water industry is responsible for the collection, treatment and supply of our water. Nuclear power is a growing industry that produces about 22 per cent of the UK's electricity.

As an apprentice in this sector, you could be working for a large combined power and gas company, an electricity company, a gas company, a water company, a combined water and waste company or a specialist contractor. A wide range of career opportunities are available, from operating and maintaining equipment in a power station to installing and servicing gas appliances in homes and businesses, or installing and maintaining mains pipes in the water network.

The skills you need will depend on the role and industry you are working in. If you are good with your hands, you may be interested in practical roles such as pipe fitting, cable jointing or operating plant and equipment. If you have an interest in mechanics, you may prefer a role where you are maintaining machinery and diagnosing and repairing faults with equipment. If you have good problem-solving skills and an interest in technology then you may choose to train in a technical role, such as a service technician in the gas industry.

You may find a role in this sector appealing if you:

- have an interest in the energy and utilities sector
- enjoy learning practical skills
- like working with your hands
- enjoy problem solving
- have an interest in maths, science or technology subjects
- like working in a team
- have an interest in mechanics and machinery.

Apprenticeships are available in the following sectors.

- Gas industry
- Nuclear decommissioning
- Power industry
- Specialised process operations (nuclear)
- Water industry

For information on the relevant Sector Skills Councils, which industries and apprenticeships they represent and web addresses where you can find out more about apprenticeships and careers, refer to Chapter 9.

Gas industry

This apprenticeship covers a range of roles in the gas industry. The term 'beach to burner' is often used to summarise the breadth of the gas industry. It primarily covers the activities associated with the transport of gas (transmission and distribution) and the fitting/maintenance of gas equipment in the customers' properties (utilisation). On this apprenticeship, you could be working in either of these sub-sectors of the gas industry.

You could be training to work in the installation, service and repair of gas appliances (such as central heating systems, boilers and gas turbines) in homes, businesses, and industrial premises. On this apprenticeship, you will learn how to safely connect appliances to gas supplies. There are pathways in either domestic natural gas installation and maintenance or in industrial and commercial gas installation and maintenance.

On this apprenticeship, you could be working for a company that provides installation and maintenance services to industrial, commercial and domestic customers. This could involve working for one of the largest energy suppliers such as British Gas or for one of the many smaller companies registered on the Gas Safety Register. (All businesses, and the people they employ to work on consumers' gas appliances, must be registered in order to work lawfully.) You would be working in a sub-sector of the UK gas industry called gas utilisation, which employs around 123,700 people.

This apprenticeship also has a pathway in gas network operations. On this, you would be working in the transmission and distribution sub-sector for a major employer such as National Grid or a specialist contractor. As an apprentice working on the gas network, you would be involved in laying and maintaining the network of gas service and main pipes across the country.

Job roles

Level 2 (Apprenticeship) roles comprise:

- trainee central heating installer
- trainee central heating maintenance engineer
- trainee domestic service engineer
- trainee industrial/commercial/catering gas installation and/or maintenance engineer
- trainee mains-layer
- trainee service-layer.

Roles at Level 3 (Advanced Apprenticeship) are:

- trainee central heating design and installation engineer
- trainee emergency service engineer
- trainee gas distribution technician
- trainee industrial/commercial/catering gas installation and/or maintenance engineer
- trainee service technician.

Work and training

On the Apprenticeship pathway in domestic natural gas installation and maintenance, you will work on the job towards an NVQ Level 2 in Domestic Natural Gas Installation and Maintenance, and off the job towards a Certificate in Domestic Natural Gas Installation and Maintenance at Level 2. On the Advanced Apprenticeship, you will work on the job towards a relevant NVQ at Level 3 and off the job towards a technical certificate at Level 3.

On both the industrial and commercial gas installation and maintenance and the gas network operations pathways, you will work on the job towards a relevant NVQ at Level 2 on the Apprenticeship and at Level 3 under the Advanced Apprenticeship.

As an apprentice, you will learn how to install and service customers' central heating systems and appliances such as gas fires and cookers. You will also learn how to diagnose, find and repair faults and how to design system upgrades to improve efficiency and flexibility.

You will also work towards registration on the Gas Safety Register. You will cover all aspects of the job, including customer service, technical quality, tools and materials. You will use a wide range of hand tools including spanners and wrenches as well as specialist plumbing tools for bending pipes and soldering joints.

On the Advanced Apprenticeship, you will be working on more complex systems. You will also have the option to follow the emergency services pathway, on which you will learn how to respond to an emergency, assess the situation and make necessary repairs.

On the gas network operations pathway, you would learn how to install and maintain the pipelines that supply millions of residential homes and businesses with gas. On this apprenticeship, you would be training to become a service-layer or a mains-layer, depending on the size of the pipes you are working with.

On the Advanced Apprenticeship, you would be training to become a gas distribution technician. You would oversee the installation and maintenance of gas network service and mains pipes throughout the country.

Entry requirements

There are no set entry requirements for the Apprenticeship and Advanced Apprenticeship and employers determine their own criteria. For the Advanced Apprenticeship, however, you will usually need at least three to five GCSEs (A*–C) including English, maths and a science subject. Applicants with GCSEs grades D–E in the same subject areas will normally be considered for an Apprenticeship.

You'll need to have problem-solving skills, a good basic knowledge of maths and enjoy manual work. It helps if you have a polite manner and good communication skills because you will be dealing regularly with customers. You will also need to be very safety-conscious.

Salary once qualified

You could earn around £16,000 to £20,000 depending on the role.

Progression

After completing the Apprenticeship, you can progress to the Advanced Apprenticeship and then on to qualifications at Level 4. The Advanced Apprenticeship provides the best preparation for achieving skilled status in the industry, as completion of the NVQ Level 3 leads to engineering technician status.

You could also progress to incorporated engineer or chartered engineer level, with further study and professional development.

Opportunities to progress in the gas industry are good, and technicians may go on to become supervisors, managers and general managers. With experience you could also set up your own business.

Power industry

This apprenticeship covers jobs in three key areas of the power industry:

1. generation – power stations and other electricity generation facilities such as wind farms
2. transmission – generated electricity flows on to the national transmission system at a high voltage via a network of overhead lines, supported by steel pylons and via underground cables
3. distribution – overhead lines and underground cables distribute electricity from the transmission network via substations to homes, factories and businesses.

For modern society to function, we need an electrical supply system that is both reliable and safe. The power industry employs tens of thousands of people, working together to keep electricity flowing into our homes. On this apprenticeship, you could be working for an electricity generation company, a transmission company, a distribution company or an electrical contractor.

Job roles

Roles in this sector are:

*   trainee cable jointer
*   trainee overhead linesperson
*   trainee electrical fitter.

Work and training

On the Apprenticeship, you will work on the job towards a Level 2 Diploma in Electrical Power Engineering and off the job towards a relevant technical certificate at Level 2.

On the Advanced Apprenticeship, you will work on the job towards a Level 3 Diploma in Electrical Power Engineering and off the job towards a relevant technical certificate at Level 3.

All areas of this apprenticeship focus on the installation and maintenance of plant and equipment associated with electricity distribution, transmission and generation. Safety is extremely important and this will be reflected in your ongoing health and safety training.

As an apprentice on the generation pathway, your work would involve the operation and maintenance of equipment in the power station. The station could produce electricity by utilising gas, coal, wind power or nuclear power. You could be using machinery and plant such as boilers and generators, diagnosing and repairing faults with equipment or carrying out routine testing.

As an apprentice on the distribution and transmission pathways, you'd be installing and maintaining the equipment and machinery that supplies electricity to homes, factories and businesses via overhead lines and underground cables. This work can involve many tasks, such as joining and repairing power cables, installing and repairing power lines and installing, repairing and maintaining equipment in electricity substations.

Entry requirements

There are no specific entry requirements for the Apprenticeship and employers set their own criteria. For the Advanced Apprenticeship you will usually need five GCSEs (A*–C), including English, maths and other relevant subjects such as science, engineering and design and technology. You will need to have normal colour vision and be very safety-conscious.

It helps if you have good practical and problem-solving skills and an interest in technology. Excellent communication skills and the ability to work either in a team or on your own are also important.

Salary once qualified

You could earn from £14,000 to £18,000 on qualification.

Progression

After completing the Apprenticeship, you may progress to the Advanced Apprenticeship in Power or work towards a Level 3 NVQ in your job. After successfully completing an Apprenticeship, and with an NVQ at Level 3, you could achieve craftsperson status.

Some employers may support you with further training, study and professional development that will allow you to progress to become an engineering technician in a supervisory post. With further study and professional development you could also progress to incorporated engineer or chartered engineer level.

Water industry

This apprenticeship covers a wide range of job roles in the water industry, involving the collection, treatment and supply of water to domestic and commercial customers.

The industry employs thousands of people across the UK to make sure water is drinkable and safe. Rain is collected and stored in reservoirs then processed at treatment works and piped to homes and businesses. After it is used, it goes into waste systems, is reprocessed and then used again. On this apprenticeship, you could be working for a large water company, a combined water and sewage company or a specialist contractor.

Job roles

At Level 2 (Apprenticeship), roles are:

- mains-layer
- plant operator
- service-layer
- sewerage process operator
- wastewater treatment plant operator
- water distribution operator
- water treatment plant operator.

Level 3 (Advanced Apprenticeship) jobs are:

- mains and services supervisor
- water bailiff
- water treatment supervisor.

Work and training

On the Apprenticeship, you will work on the job towards a relevant qualification at Level 2. There are different pathways in the Apprenticeship framework and the qualification you take will depend on your particular role. You will also work off the job towards a Level 2 Certificate in Water Engineering.

On the Advanced Apprenticeship, you will work on the job towards a relevant NVQ at Level 3 and off the job towards a Level 3 Certificate in Water Engineering.

On the Apprenticeship, you could be working as a water distribution officer, operating and managing the water network on a daily basis. You could work as a plant operator, supporting the processes at the treatment plant. Your duties will depend on the area in which you specialise, for example water treatment or wastewater treatment, but you could be operating, monitoring and maintaining a wide range of plant and apparatus.

As a mains-layer you will be repairing, maintaining and installing mains pipes in the water network on a day-to-day basis. This could involve planned maintenance, such as replacing damaged pipes, or responding to customer call-outs and emergencies, such as burst mains pipes.

On the Advanced Apprenticeship, you may take on a more supervisory role, As a water treatment supervisor, for example, you would be managing and supervising water treatment operators. As a mains and service supervisor you would be overseeing mains-layers and service-layers. You may learn how to work with chemicals, detect leaks and to diagnose faults.

Entry requirements

There are no set entry requirements for the Apprenticeship and Advanced Apprenticeship and employers decide their own criteria. For the Advanced Apprenticeship, however, you will usually need at least three to five GCSEs (A*–C) including English, maths and a science subject. Applicants with GCSEs at grades D–E in the same subject areas will normally be considered for an Apprenticeship.

It helps if you are physically fit with good practical skills and enjoy solving problems. An interest in mechanics is also useful for those working with machinery.

Salary once qualified

Your salary could be around £17,000 after qualification.

Progression

After completing the Apprenticeship, you can progress to the Advanced Apprenticeship and then to an NVQ at Level 4 or higher education, such as a Foundation degree or possibly a degree in engineering or environmental sciences. The Advanced Apprenticeship provides the best preparation for achieving skilled status in the industry.

There are good opportunities in the water industry to progress to team leader, supervisory and management positions. Further qualifications, such as a degree, could allow you to progress to higher technical positions.

There may also be opportunities for overseas work, particularly in developing countries.

ENGINEERING AND MANUFACTURING TECHNOLOGIES

Engineering is about making things work. The engineering industry deals with designing, producing and maintaining the machinery and systems we use in everyday life, from aeroplanes and cars to computers and telecommunications systems. The engineering industry is huge, employing 1.28 million people in a range of sub-sectors from aerospace and automotive to electrical equipment and electronics.

Manufacturing is about making things – using machines, tools and labour. Nearly everything we use or consume in our everyday lives has been manufactured. The UK manufacturing sector is huge, employing around 2.2 million people in a range of industries. Some of the main manufacturing industries are food, furniture, glass, textiles, metals and printing.

As an apprentice in this sector, you could be working for a large multinational company or a small local firm. In such a broad sector there is a wide range of career opportunities. On an Apprenticeship in Engineering, you could be working in a wide range of job roles, from assembling radios, TVs and computers to fitting aeroplane or car engines, or maintaining and servicing lifts and escalators. In manufacturing, you could train to become a sewing machinist, cabinet maker, machine printer or windscreen fitter, for example.

The motor industry is an important part of engineering (for more information on apprenticeships and job roles in the motor industry, have a look at the Vehicles and Transport section). There are also engineering roles in the energy and utilities sector (see the preceding section for more information).

The skills you need will depend on the role and industry you are working in. If you enjoy practical and manual work then you may be interested in one of the many operative roles in the sector. For these roles, you will need to be able to work in a team and follow instructions, as well as having a reasonable level of fitness.

In many jobs, an Apprenticeship will teach you craft skills and technical knowledge. If you have good problem-solving skills and like to work with technology, then you may choose to train in a technician role on an Advanced Apprenticeship, learning how to deal with more complex technical problems.

You may be interested in a role in this sector if you:

- enjoy learning practical skills
- enjoy working in a team
- like working with your hands
- like working with tools and machinery
- have an interest in maths, technology or science subjects
- are enthusiastic about developing technologies
- like solving problems.

Apprenticeships in this sector are available in the following areas.

- Building products occupations
- Ceramics manufacturing
- Coating operations
- Engineering
- Engineering construction
- Engineering technology
- Extractive and mineral processing operations
- Food manufacture
- Furniture, furnishings and interiors manufacturing industry
- Glass industry occupations
- Industrial applications
- Laboratory technicians
- Marine industry
- Metal processing
- Paper and board manufacture
- Polymer processing and sign-making
- Print and printed packaging
- Process technology
- Sea fishing

For information on the relevant Sector Skills Councils, which industries and apprenticeships they represent and important web links with more about apprenticeships and careers in this sector refer to Chapter 9.

Ceramics manufacturing

On this Apprenticeship, you will learn about the manufacture of ceramics and associated products. Ceramic items are made from clay, which is extracted from the ground and processed. The liquid clay is then moulded into shape, decorated, glazed and heated at a high temperature to harden it.

Ceramic items that are manufactured range from industrial items such as bricks, roof tiles, drains and pipes to domestic items such as cups, plates and bowls, floor and wall tiles and baths, basins and toilets. Ceramic components are also used in sectors such as the aerospace and automotive industries.

The ceramics sector employs around 16,000 people in some 700 companies. Many of the larger manufacturers are based in the West Midlands. On this Apprenticeship, you could be working at businesses from large manufacturers to small pottery workshops.

Job roles
Apprenticeships are available as a:

- ceramic maker
- decorator.

Work and training
On this Apprenticeship, you will work on the job towards NVQ Level 2 Manufacturing Ceramic and Associated Products, and off the job towards a Level 2 Certificate in Ceramics Manufacturing. You will start your Apprenticeship in one particular occupation in the industry. You will then learn about the whole ceramics manufacturing process, looking at what other occupations exist – including, for example, deco-machine operator, hand

painter, sponge decorator, dish-maker and kiln operative – and where your role fits into the supply chain.

Some manufacturing processes are partly or fully automated, while others are carried out by hand. Depending on your role, you will follow one of two pathways: the hand-led route or the performing manufacturing operations route. You will also learn about customer care and quality assurance, and may receive specific health and safety training.

There is a wide range of jobs available in ceramics manufacturing. As an apprentice you could be:

- preparing and processing materials
- making products from clay by hand or machine
- hand painting
- applying patterns to ceramic products
- processing products using computer-controlled equipment
- inspecting and quality-assuring finished pieces.

You are likely to learn more than one skill, both during your apprenticeship and after you have completed the programme.

Entry requirements

There are no set entry requirements, although you will need to demonstrate you have the ability to complete the programme. Employers look for candidates with team-working skills and the ability to follow instructions and who are enthusiastic and willing to adapt to different roles. It helps if you are good with your hands and enjoy practical work.

Salary once qualified

You could earn around £10,000 on qualification.

Progression

Successful apprentices may go on to take further NVQs, for example Team Leader NVQ at Level 2 and Level 3, or NVQs in customer care. They may go on to higher education, for example to a Foundation degree in management.

Ceramic workers may progress to team leader, supervisor, line manager, trainer or technician roles, especially if they have gained relevant qualifications. It may be possible to become self-employed, setting up your own craft studio or workshop.

Engineering

The engineering industry in the UK is huge, designing, producing and maintaining the machinery, products and systems we use in everyday life from aeroplanes and hospital medical equipment to computers and telecommunications systems. It offers a huge range of career opportunities across a range of sub-sectors.

The core engineering sub-sectors are:

- aerospace
- automotive
- basic metals
- electrical equipment
- electronics
- other transport equipment
- mechanical equipment
- shipbuilding.

On this apprenticeship, you could be working for a diverse range of employers, from machinery manufacturers and steel-makers to hi-tech manufacturing companies in the aerospace or computing industries. You could be working for a large multinational or a small local firm.

Job roles

Job roles at Level 2 (Apprenticeship) are broken down into the following pathways.

Performing engineering operations

- Aero-engine fitter (semi-skilled)
- Computer-aided design (CAD) operator
- Cycle maintenance mechanic
- Electrical fitter's mate
- Electronics service rep
- Engineering fitter (semi-skilled)
- Motorsport technician
- Production operator
- Repair technician
- Welder/fabricator's mate

Business improvement techniques

- Production process control operator

Mechanical manufacturing engineering

- Aero-engine fitter (semi-skilled)
- Fitter's mate (air conditioning manufacture)
- Line maintenance fitter (electrical/electronics)
- Manufacturing expeditor
- Manufacturing operator
- Production CAD programmer
- Production planner
- Quality control operator
- Welder/fabricator (semi-skilled)

Fabrication and welding engineering

- Computer numerical control (CNC) cutter
- CNC fabrication operator
- Jig welder
- Military vehicle fitter/welder (semi-skilled)
- Production control operator
- Production fabricator (semi-skilled)
- Vehicle body repair technician
- Welding equipment maintenance fitter (semi-skilled)
- Welding inspector

Aeronautical engineering

- Aero-engine component assembly
- Aero-engine fitter/tester's mate
- Aero-engine strip and wash fitter
- Airframe riveter
- CNC operator
- Welder/fabricator aero-engine pipework
- Workflow control operator

Instrument servicing

- Automotive instrument repairer
- Avionics instrument calibration technician
- Instrument fabricator (semi-skilled)
- Instrument repair fitter electrical/electronics (semi-skilled)
- Manufacturing calibration control technician
- Metrology operator
- Repair of instruments and control systems – military vehicles
- Watch service technician

Engineering maintenance and installation

- Commissioned fitter (semi-skilled)
- Cycle maintenance technician
- Lift control systems maintenance engineer
- Maintenance welder (semi-skilled)
- Military vehicle fitter (semi-skilled)
- Planned maintenance controller
- Plant fitter heating and ventilation (semi-skilled)
- Plant maintenance fitter's mate
- Plant maintenance planner

Roles at Level 3 (Advanced Apprenticeship) are as follows:

- aircraft service engineer (unlicensed)
- electronics systems maintenance engineer

- facilities maintenance engineer
- facilities manager
- maintenance controller
- maintenance welder (skilled)
- manufacturing maintenance engineer
- micro electronics maintenance engineer
- plant maintenance engineer
- repair and overhaul engineer (aircraft engines)
- specialist vehicle maintenance engineer
- systems maintenance engineer (hydraulics, pneumatics)
- telecommunications maintenance/service engineer
- watchmaker/clockmaker.

Work and training

As you can see above, both the Apprenticeship and Advanced Apprenticeship frameworks cover a vast range of job roles and functions. There is therefore a wide range of qualifications available under both frameworks to reflect various pathways, and the qualifications you take will depend on the sector you are working in and your particular role.

On the Apprenticeship and Advanced Apprenticeship you will work on the job towards a relevant NVQ and off the job towards a relevant technical certificate, at Level 2 and Level 3 respectively. On both programmes you will also take Performing Engineering Operations NVQ Level 2, which provides skills in essential health and safety and basic engineering.

Your duties will vary depending on your employer. On the Apprenticeship, however, you will generally be learning an operator role in one area of engineering. Engineering operatives are involved in the manufacture and production of a huge variety of products and services, such as assembling components into finished products, fitting parts to machinery and equipment, operating machine tools such as lathes and grinders or maintaining equipment and machinery. You could also learn practical skills such as welding, fabrication, general maintenance and other engineering applications.

On the Advanced Apprenticeship, you could train to become a skilled craftsperson carrying out a specific highly skilled craft occupation, for example, fitting or machining. Alternatively, you could train to become a technician, learning how to apply your knowledge and technical abilities to solve practical problems. You could learn how to produce and interpret complex engineering drawings. You may learn specific skills such as CAD, mechanical engineering and CNC programming.

Entry requirements

There are no specific entry requirements because employers set their own criteria, and as such these vary. However, if you are considering an Apprenticeship then you should usually have three to five GCSEs at grades D–G, including English, maths and a science.

Case Study

Ed Wilson

Ed is on an Advanced Apprenticeship in Engineering.

'I always knew I wanted to do engineering. When I was younger, my brother and I were always taking things apart, like lawnmower engines, and then putting them back together to see if they would work again. We made soap boxes and built a kit car with my dad, which made me think about working on bigger machines.

'At school. I did well in my GCSEs and decided to take A levels to keep my options open. I took maths and mechanics, design and technology and geography, and an AS Level in physics. I was applying to engineering degree courses when I heard that a local factory was advertising for apprentices. My brother is with the same employer and he's on the final year of his apprenticeship so he told me about it, but it was also advertised in the local press and in the sixth-form common room. I decided to choose the apprenticeship route as I wanted to be more practical rather than classroom-based. My dad was an agricultural engineer and he started out as an apprentice, so I guess it's become a family trend now.

'My apprenticeship will take four years to complete. I've already gained NVQ Level 2 in Performing Engineering Operations and am now working towards an NVQ at Level 3 and a BTEC National Certificate. I spent the first year full-time at college, which involved practical work and studying towards qualifications. I now come into college one day a week.

'My apprenticeship scheme is very structured and well organised. During the first year at work, apprentices are based in the central workshops. I'm working with the machinists at the moment, who make new components such as cams for the conveyors. At college, we made pieces to show our skills, but I like the fact that I'm actually out there working for something now, making parts for the machines. The work is practical but also involves communication – for example with the stores over the parts we need.

'After this year, I'll spend the next two years getting experience in the factory's different departments and be set specific tasks to work towards. As apprentices, we learn skills in both mechanical and electrical engineering, which is called dual-skilling, and is more viable for the employer as we can work in different areas.

'After the Advanced Apprenticeship I will be a qualified plant technician. I will also be able to go on to take a Foundation degree, followed by a degree, and end up at the same point academically as I would if I'd gone to university straight after A levels. I'm really glad I chose to do an apprenticeship. I'm getting paid, getting experience in industry and still learning. I'd like to stay with my present employer – who would sponsor me to get higher qualifications – and aim as high as I can get.'

If you are seeking an Advanced Apprenticeship then entry requirements are usually four to five GCSEs at grades A*–C, including English and maths. The Diploma in Engineering may also be relevant.

It helps if you have an interest in science, technology and solving problems. Maths, communication and ICT skills are valuable, and you will need good manual skills. Engineering is a team activity too, so you will need to be able to work well with others.

Salary once qualified
Depending on the role, you could earn £12,000 to £20,000.

Progression
The Apprenticeship provides the best preparation for achieving trained operator/semi-skilled status in the industry. After completing the Apprenticeship, you can progress to the Advanced Apprenticeship, which helps prepare you for skilled craft and/or technician status in the industry.

Advanced Apprenticeships in turn provide progression opportunities to higher education, such as a Foundation degree or degree or a Higher Apprenticeship. A Higher Apprenticeship incorporates a Foundation degree and an NVQ at Level 3 or 4. It develops engineering technicians for a variety of job roles and functions, including design, development, engineering manufacture, quality assurance, maintenance, testing, commissioning and so on.

Technicians can go on to achieve accredited engineering technician status with a professional engineering institute. With further study and experience, they may progress to incorporated engineer or chartered engineer level.

Engineering technicians and craftspeople have the option to follow various career routes, including engineering, management or project management, and former engineering apprentices can be found at all levels in a company, including top management roles.

Furniture, furnishings and interiors manufacturing industry

This apprenticeship covers a wide range of job roles in the design, manufacture, production and installation of furniture. It is aimed at people interested in working in the furniture, furnishings and interiors industry. On this apprenticeship, you could be based in a small workshop or in a big factory where large automated machinery is used.

The furniture, furnishing and interiors industry employs around 150,000 people in the UK and is made up of three sub-sectors:

1. domestic – serving the public directly and through retail outlets
2. office – desks, seating, tables and other items for the workplace
3. contract – furniture and furnishings for public buildings such as hotels and airports.

Businesses in these sub-sectors produce a variety of furnishings from upholstered products (such as settees) to furniture for bedrooms, kitchens and living rooms, as well as soft furnishings such as cushion covers and curtains.

Job roles

Roles in the industry are:

- cabinet-making
- curtain and blind design and manufacture
- furniture assembly
- furniture component manufacture
- furniture design (including home office, commercial office, curtains and blinds)
- furniture installation (including kitchen, bedroom, bathroom and soft furnishings)
- furniture restoration (upholstered and cabinet)
- garden and leisure furniture design and manufacture
- kitchen, bedroom and bathroom unit manufacture
- kitchen/bedroom design
- kitchen/bedroom installation
- office and contract furniture assembly
- polishing and finishing (including French polishing)
- soft furnishing design and manufacture
- upholstery
- upholstery cutting
- upholstery sewing
- veneering
- restoration and repair
- wood machining.

Work and training

On the Apprenticeship, you will work on the job towards a relevant NVQ at Level 2 and off the job towards a Level 2 Certificate in Furniture Production. The NVQ you choose will depend on your job role. At NVQ Level 2, the following pathways are available:

- fitted interiors
- making and installing furniture
- wood machining.

On the Advanced Apprenticeship, you will work on the job towards a relevant NVQ at Level 3 and off the job towards a Level 3 Certificate in Furniture Production. At NVQ Level 3, the following pathways are available:

- making and repairing hand-crafted furniture and furnishings
- making and installing production furniture
- wood machining.

On this apprenticeship, you will develop skills using your hands and specialist equipment while learning about furniture materials and production methods.

Your particular duties will depend on your employer and job role.

As a cabinet-maker, for example, you would be producing and assembling components for furniture such as dining room tables and chests of drawers. As a polisher and finisher, you would prepare and treat wood to give it a smooth finish. As an upholsterer you could be covering or re-covering furniture with fabric. Alternatively, you could be working in production, helping to manufacture items, in installation, helping to install kitchens and bathrooms, or in a design role.

Entry requirements

There are no set entry requirements for the Apprenticeship or the Advanced Apprenticeship and employers devise their own criteria. But you will need to be able to demonstrate you have the ability to complete the programme. You may have an initial assessment, a practical observation and literacy and numeracy tests. Employers look for a good basic education, including literacy and numeracy skills. They may prefer GCSEs (A*–G) in subjects such as English, maths, ICT, science and design and technology.

You should have an interest in making furniture, furnishings and interiors and like working with your hands. To work in the production side of the industry you will need good hand–eye coordination. The ability to use tools effectively, a quality-driven approach and team working skills are highly valued. It also helps if you have a reasonable level of fitness.

Salary once qualified

On qualification, you could earn upwards of £14,000.

Progression

On completion of the Apprenticeship, you will gain full operative status in the industry. It may then be possible to progress to the Advanced Apprenticeship, and then into higher education such as a relevant Foundation degree or higher-level NVQs or professional qualifications.

Progression is possible to supervisory and higher levels, with many companies promoting staff from within. Typical progression may be to team leader then junior management, and on to senior management roles. It may also be possible to set up your own business as an independent craftsperson, such as an antique furniture restorer or a bespoke cabinet-maker.

Glass industry occupations

This apprenticeship deals with the manufacture and process of glass and related products. As an apprentice in this field, you'll either be working on the manufacturing side of things – with 'hot-end' molten glass processes – or with the finished products once the glass is cold, for example, the installation of glass windows and doors. You could either be working in a large industrial factory setting, in a small craft workshop, on domestic housing or on commercial construction sites.

Around 2.8 millions of tonnes of glass are produced each year in the UK. The glass manufacturing sector in the UK employs around 33,000 people and the glazing industries around 100,000.

The glass industry occupations apprenticeship framework is broken down into the following areas:

- automotive sector – windscreens, lights, mirrors, sunroofs etc.
- container glass production – bottles, jars, light bulbs, drinking glasses etc.
- conservatory installation – the manufacture of plastic, wood and aluminium conservatories, custom-made for domestic and commercial purposes
- crystal glass and tableware – decanters, flasks, vases, stained glass etc.
- fibreglass production – insulation, optical cables and reinforcing of cement, plastics and rubber
- flat glass production and processing – toughening, laminating or curving glass for mirrors, windows and doors etc.
- scientific glass – optical glass, including microscopes, telescopes, spectacles etc.
- window and door fabrication and installation – the manufacture of windows and doors and their installation in private houses and large public buildings, as well as the construction of major glass structures.

Job roles

Roles at Level 2 (Apprenticeship) are:

- automotive glazier/windscreen fitter and repairer
- fabricator/frame-maker
- glass-maker/operator/manufacturer
- glass processor
- glazier, installer, fitter, glazing systems maintainer
- installer/fitter
- roofline installer.

Level 3 (Advanced Apprenticeship) roles comprise:

- automotive glazier/technician/fitter/leading hand/team leader
- fabricator/frame-maker
- glazier, installer, fitter, glazing systems maintainer
- installer/surveyor, controller/technician, glass processor.

Work and training

On this Apprenticeship, you will work on the job towards a relevant NVQ at Level 2 and off the job towards a Level 2 Certificate in Glass-related Occupations. You will be dealing with routine assignments. On the Advanced Apprenticeship, you will work on the job towards a relevant NVQ at Level 3 and off the job towards a Level 3 Certificate in Glass-Related Occupations. You will have technical supervisory responsibilities in your role and contribute to the quality assurance and control procedures, including safety, production, quality, waste and customer service.

On the Apprenticeship, you could be working as an automotive glazier or windscreen fitter and repairer in the replacement automotive glazing industry. You would be repairing or replacing glazing components in standard motor vehicles. You could be working on the roadside or in fixed sites. As a glazier, you would be installing glass into window and door frames, for example, and as an installer/fitter you would be installing glass-supporting systems, such as replacement windows and doors, on customer premises.

As a glass-maker/operator/manufacturer in a factory, you would be working with raw materials, melted glass materials or semi-finished products. Your work could include receiving and batching raw materials before they are processed or controlling heating equipment to melt and form glass from the raw materials. As a glass processor, you would manufacture products from glass and related materials. This could involve cutting, shaping, assembling and finishing the products, the latter including decoration.

On the Advanced Apprenticeship as an automotive glazier/technician/team leader, you would be dealing with a wide range of issues, including working with vehicles that have more complex problems, such as old or expensive vehicles where parts are hard to obtain. You will work closely with customers and develop your customer service skills. You will often take a technical oversight role, supervising less experienced automotive glaziers.

Entry requirements

There are no set entry requirements and employers determine their own criteria. For the Apprenticeship, you will need to be able to demonstrate that you can complete the programme. Employers may look for three or more GCSEs grades A*–G in English, maths and science. For the Advanced Apprenticeship, you shoud ideally have achieved a Level 2 practical qualification.

Many glass/glazing jobs involve manual skills, and it helps if you enjoy working with your hands and have a reasonable level of physical fitness. Team working and communication skills are also useful.

Salary once qualified

You could earn £14,000 to £18,000 on qualification.

Progression

After completing the Apprenticeship, you will have trained status in the glass industry and you could progress to the Advanced Apprenticeship or higher level work. The Advanced Apprenticeship provides the best preparation for achieving technical, skilled or supervisory status in the industry. There are opportunities to progress into supervisory or management roles.

Following the Advanced Apprenticeship, it may be possible to progress to higher education such as a relevant Foundation degree, higher-level NVQs or professional qualifications.

Marine industry

This apprenticeship covers a range of occupations in the marine industry dealing with the manufacture, repair and servicing of boats – from large luxury power and sailing boats through to narrowboats and small wooden dinghies.

On this apprenticeship, you could be working for a major boat builder, a smaller boatyard or marina, a small engine manufacturer or an inland waterways hire fleet.

Job roles

At Level 2 (Apprenticeship), you could work as a:

- boat builder
- laminator
- marine electrician
- marine engineer.

Level 3 (Advanced Apprenticeship) roles are:

- boat builder
- carpenter
- marine electrician
- marine engineer.

Work and training

The marine apprenticeship has pathways in the following occupations:

- boat building, maintenance and repair
- electrics and electronics
- engineering maintenance
- marine engineering.

On the Apprenticeship, you will work on the job towards a relevant NVQ at Level 2 and off the job towards the Level 2 Certificate in Boat Production, Maintenance and Support. You will be working under supervision in a supporting role and learning basic skills such as interpreting drawings and selecting materials and hand tools. You may be working for a small company taking on a range of tasks, such as boat handling, repair and outfitting.

On the Advanced Apprenticeship you will work on the job towards a relevant NVQ at Level 3 and off the job towards the Certificate in Boat Production, Maintenance and Support at Level 3. You will be working as a craftsperson on a range of more complex tasks without direct supervision.

On the boat building pathway, you might learn a variety of relevant skills including carpentry and electrical, plumbing and welding skills as well as traditional maritime techniques such as rigging and sail-making. Your work could involve constructing frameworks, hulls and decks: boat building takes on several different forms. Most modern boats are built using fibreglass or new composite materials in a factory environment. However, there are also specialist craftspeople who build traditional wooden boats or steel narrowboats. There is also a need for repair and restoration of existing wooden boats.

As a carpenter, you would be responsible for making and fitting internal accommodation, such as cabinets, lockers and furniture.

Working in electrics and electronics, you would be dealing with sophisticated electrical and electronic systems, ranging from engine electrical systems to radar and satellite navigation and communications equipment. You would learn how to install, service, repair and upgrade these.

As a marine engineer, you would learn the practical and technical skills needed to install, service and repair engines. You could be working on anything from petrol engines in high-performance sports boats to diesel engine installations in motor cruisers and yachts.

Entry requirements

There are no set entry requirements for the Apprenticeship and Advanced Apprenticeship, although you will need to demonstrate that you can complete the programme. For the Apprenticeship, you should ideally have GCSEs in English and maths and for the Advanced Apprenticeship, five GCSEs at grade C or above (or have completed the Apprenticeship). However, these are not mandatory requirements.

It helps if you are good with your hands, enjoy practical work and have an interest in technology and problem solving.

Salary once qualified

You could earn from £12,000 to £17,000 having completed your apprenticeship.

Progression

On completion of the Apprenticeship, you can progress to the Advanced Apprentice-ship. This will provide you with the best preparation for achieving skilled craft and technician status in the industry.

After the Advanced Apprenticeship, you can go into higher-level work such as a supervisory position and from there into management in a technical or related role, such as project management. You may also be able to progress to higher education such as a Foundation degree.

Boat building and repair also offer you the chance to become self-employed.

Print and printed packaging

This apprenticeship covers a range of jobs in the printing industry, from operating specialist machinery to book-binding and graphic design. You could be working in a factory for a large printing company, a small high street print shop or a design studio.

The printing industry is an essential part of the UK's economy, employing over 160,000 people in more than 16,000 companies. It serves all areas of business and leisure with a vast range of products including newspapers, books, magazines, money, printed packaging and signage. Demand for printed products continues to grow. Many print companies are now expanding their services into graphic design, marketing, web design and/or advertising.

Job roles

At Level 2 (Apprenticeship), roles are as follows:

- digital print production – e.g. scanning technician, proofing technician, pre-press technician, plate-maker, desktop publisher, graphic designer, print designer
- envelope printer
- machine printer
- mechanised print finisher and binder – e.g. guillotine operator, folding machine operator, binding machine operator.

At Level 3 (Advanced Apprenticeship), you might be a:

- carton manufacturer – e.g. printed carton operative, carton die-maker
- lead digital print production printer/designer
- lead envelope printer
- lead machine printer
- lead mechanised print finisher and binder – e.g. print finisher supervisor
- print manager and administrator – e.g. account manager, internal sales administrator, sales executive, estimator, costing clerk, print production manager, print production scheduler.

Work and training

On the Apprenticeship, you will work on the job towards a relevant NVQ at Level 2 and off the job towards a Level 2 Certificate in Printing and Graphic Communication. The NVQ you take will depend on your job role. There are pathways in:

- digital print production
- envelope manufacture
- machine printing
- mechanised print finishing and binding.

On the Advanced Apprenticeship, you will work on the job towards a relevant NVQ at Level 3 and off the job towards a Level 3 Certificate in Printing and Graphic Communication. Under the NVQ at Level 3, as well as the above pathways there are additional routes in carton manufacture and in print management and administration. Your role will include technical supervisory responsibilities.

Depending on your job role, you may also receive additional skills-based training in areas such as engineering, management, customer services, business administration, ICT, quality and first aid.

On the machine printing pathway, you would be using printing presses to produce printed materials such as books, magazines, brochures and stationery. You will need to prepare, set up and operate a press and your primary role will be its safe operation.

If you are on the mechanised print finishing and binding pathway, you could be operating a machine that cuts or folds paper or one that binds printed material together to make books.

On the digital print production pathway, you could be working as a desktop publisher, using software to prepare and assemble the layout for magazines and other publications. Or you could have a graphic design role, creating illustrations and designs for books, magazines, advertising, packaging or other purposes.

Entry requirements

There are no specific entry requirements and employers set their own criteria. For the Apprenticeship, you will need to be able to demonstrate that you have the ability to complete the programme. Employers may look for three or more GCSEs, with at least grades A*–G in English, maths and science. For the Advanced Apprenticeship, you should ideally have completed the Apprenticeship, or have GCSEs in maths and English at grade C or above plus two others at grade D or equivalent; alternatively, you should have a good level of relevant industry experience.

It helps if you have good communication and number skills, good problem-solving abilities, are a team player and enthusiastic about developing technologies. For desktop publishing and graphic design roles, creativity is essential.

Salary once qualified

You could earn £16,000 or upwards once you have qualified.

Progression

On completing the Apprenticeship, you will gain trained status in the printing industry and may be able to progress onto the Advanced Apprenticeship or higher-level work.

The Advanced Apprenticeship is the best preparation for achieving technical, skilled or supervisory status in the industry. There are then opportunities to progress to supervisory or management roles.

Following the Advanced Apprenticeship, it may be possible to progress to higher education such as a relevant Foundation degree, or on to higher-level NVQs or professional qualifications.

ENVIRONMENTAL AND LAND-BASED INDUSTRIES

At present, the environment and land-based sector employs over 1.1 million people in the UK. As technology advances in the sector, the opportunities continue to grow. Lantra, the relevant Sector Skills Council, has estimated that 215,000 new workers will be needed in the next ten years to meet the demands of this dynamic sector.

The sector itself comprises 17 different industries, from agricultural livestock and floristry to animal care and environmental conservation. They can be grouped broadly into:

- animal health and welfare
- environmental industries
- land management and production.

Each of the industries offers you the chance to develop skills in practical, technical and specialised areas. There is a wide range of career opportunities available in different working environments, from farms and wildlife parks to floristry and horticulture businesses. As an apprentice, you could be training, for example, to become a farm worker, fencing contractor, gardener, ranger/countryside officer, gamekeeper, tree surgeon, stable-hand or zoo keeper.

Practical skills are important in this sector and many jobs require physical work. But there's a demand for creative talent, too, in jobs such as floristry and garden design, and caring roles such as a veterinary assistant or zoo keeper.

If you want to get on, there are plenty of opportunities to progress into managerial roles, and if you're interested in being your own boss it's worth noting that more than half the people in this sector are self-employed.

You may be interested in a role in this sector if you:

- like working with plants or animals
- like the opportunity to work outdoors
- like working with and applying new technology
- want to make a difference to the environment we live in
- enjoy responsibility and being part of a small team
- enjoy learning practical skills
- enjoy physical work.

Apprenticeships are available in the following sectors.

- Agriculture
- Animal care
- Environmental conservation
- Equine industry
- Farriery
- Fencing
- Floristry

- Game and wildlife management
- Horticulture
- Land-based engineering
- Trees and timber
- Veterinary nursing.

Lantra has two websites where you can find out more about apprenticeships and careers in this sector (see the web addresses in Chapter 9).

Agriculture

This apprenticeship covers roles in the agricultural industry, offering a wide range of opportunities to work on livestock, crop or mixed farms. Farms vary enormously, from small hill farms to large crop farms. As an apprentice in the livestock industry, you could be working in areas such as dairy and beef cattle, sheep, pigs or poultry. As an apprentice in the crops industry, you might be growing from vegetables and cereals to energy crops. You would also be responsible for managing the land in an environmentally-friendly and sustainable way.

There are 60,700 crops businesses and around 174,800 livestock businesses in the UK. The agricultural industry is generally made up of small businesses, therefore each employee has an important role to play and agricultural workers need to develop a variety of skills.

Job roles

Roles at Level 2 (Apprenticeship) are:

- assistant stockperson
- calf rearer
- general farm/agricultural worker
- lambing assistant
- sheep shearer
- tractor driver
- vegetable grower.

Level 3 (Advanced Apprenticeship) roles comprise:

- combine driver/head combine driver
- smallholder
- sprayer operator
- stockperson/dairy person
- technician
- unit supervisor (finishing unit for pigs, beef cattle or poultry).

Work and training

In this apprenticeship, you could learn about plant care, maintenance and growing, or about animal health and welfare. You may also gain business management skills in sales, customer care, marketing, promotion and accounts. You will be progressing towards a work-based diploma, delivered through both on- and off-the-job learning. You will need to take a one-day course in emergency first aid, plus an occupational test relevant to your industry. These tests are required when operating specific pieces of machinery, using pesticides or working safely. Examples are:

- safe use of pesticides
- safe use of sheep dips
- safe use of veterinary medicines
- tractor driving
- driving with a trailer
- chainsaw maintenance and operation
- transport of animals by road
- pollution prevention control
- sheep shearing.

As an apprentice, you'll choose from a number of pathways:

- crop production
- livestock production
- mixed farming
- poultry production.

The nature of the work depends on your employer and the pathways you choose.

As a general farm worker on a livestock farm, you could be ensuring the welfare of animals, providing feed and water and monitoring their health. On a crop farm, you could be helping to plant crops, monitoring their growth and watching for diseases. As an assistant stockperson, you are likely to be working on a livestock farm looking after the cows, sheep or pigs. Your work could include milking cows, helping to shear sheep or moving pigs. Apprentices at Level 2 work towards the Level 2 Diploma in Work-based Agriculture.

On the Advanced Apprenticeship, you'll learn more specialised skills. As a stockperson/dairyperson you will be working towards having responsibility for the livestock. On a dairy farm, for example, you could be monitoring the cows during lactation, planning the breeding cycles and milking. As a sprayer operator you would learn how to maintain and clean the tractor and sprayer and how to apply pesticides. Apprentices at Level 3 work towards the Level 3 Diploma in Work-based Agriculture.

Entry requirements

There are no set entry requirements for the Apprenticeship. However, you will be assessed to make sure you're able to complete the programme. For an Advanced Apprenticeship, you'll need to hold the Level 2 Diploma in Work-based Agriculture or an equivalent qualification or have gained a lot of practical experience.

It is important to care about the environment and promoting good husbandry (raising livestock), health and welfare. It also helps if you are practical and enjoy solving problems and working outdoors.

Salary once qualified

Agricultural workers are paid at specific rates as defined in the Wages Order of the Agricultural Wages Board.

Progression

Work on larger farms offers the opportunity to specialise in a particular area, such as unit supervisor or tractor driver. There are opportunities to progress into areas linked to the agriculture industry, such as sales, research and policy development. Self-employment is also possible, for example running your own farm as a smallholder.

With an Advanced Apprenticeship, you could progress to further and higher education programmes such as an NVQ Level 4 or a Foundation degree, or continue your development through relevant industry training or certificates.

Animal care

The animal care industry offers a range of opportunities in handling, supervising and caring for animals, from small domestic pets to wildlife and zoo animals. As an apprentice, you could be working in a large kennels or cattery, for an animal charity, a pet shop or dog-grooming business, or at a wildlife park or zoo. There are also opportunities with dog trainers and pet breeders. You will learn the skills and knowledge to work at different levels of animal care.

There are currently around 13,300 animal care businesses in the UK. Pet ownership is predicted to grow and therefore the number of businesses is likely to increase.

Job roles

At Level 2 (Apprenticeship), roles are:

- animal trainer assistant
- animal technician
- assistant dog groomer
- junior zoo/animal keeper
- kennel/cattery assistant
- kennel worker
- pet shop assistant/retail assistant.

Level 3 (Advanced Apprenticeship) positions comprise:

- animal welfare supervisor
- dog groomer
- dog trainer
- inspector
- zoo/animal keeper.

Work and training

You will learn on the job about promoting and maintaining the health and well-being of animals. On the Apprenticeship you will work under supervision, while on the Advanced

Apprenticeship you will take on more of a supervisory or specialised role. You will progress towards a work-based diploma, normally delivered on the job. You will also need to take a one-day course in emergency first aid. Particular health and safety training may be required for different areas of work.

On the Apprenticeship, you'll choose between a number of pathways:

- animal care and welfare
- animal training
- dog grooming
- pet care and retail
- zoos/wildlife establishments.

On the Advanced Apprenticeship, there are further pathways in:

- animals in education and entertainment
- animal welfare enforcement
- dog/animal wardens.

The nature of the work will depend on your employer and the pathway you choose.

As an assistant dog groomer, you could help bathe, shampoo, dry and clip hair, trimming and brushing a variety of long- and short-coated dogs. As an assistant in a pet shop you would learn to care for and sell pets and pet products, as well as advising customers. As a junior zoo/animal keeper you might be cleaning and maintaining enclosures, preparing food and feeding animals and caring for those that may be ill or injured. As an apprentice at Level 2, you would work towards the Level 2 Diploma in Work-based Animal Care.

As a dog trainer, you would be working with dogs and their owners or handlers. You would learn how to teach people to handle, groom and examine dogs correctly and train their dogs to obey commands. As an inspector, you are likely to be investigating cases of animal cruelty and neglect, inspecting events and establishments where animals are kept and rescuing injured or trapped animals. On the Advanced Apprenticeship, you would work towards the Level 3 Diploma in Work-based Animal Care.

Entry requirements

There are no set entry requirements for an Apprenticeship. However, you will be assessed before starting the programme to make sure you're able to complete the programme. For an Advanced Apprenticeship, you will need to hold the Level 2 Diploma in Work-based Animal Care or an equivalent qualification, or have plenty of relevant work experience before starting the programme.

It is important to be passionate about animal welfare and have a positive attitude to learning. It also helps if you are reliable and self-motivated, confident with animals and a good communicator.

Salary once qualified

You could earn between £10,000 and £14,000 depending on your role.

Progression

There are good opportunities, for example at large boarding kennels and zoos, to progress into management roles. Many dog groomers and trainers become self-employed and run their own businesses. With an Advanced Apprenticeship, you could progress to further and higher education programmes such as an NVQ Level 4 or a Foundation degree, or develop your career through relevant industry training.

Environmental conservation

This Apprenticeship covers roles in the conservation of rural and urban landscapes, birds, animals and plants, and waterways. Environmental conservation offers opportunities in areas such as habitat management, countryside recreation, planning and parks, and the protection of animals and plants. As an apprentice, you could be working for a government department or in the voluntary sector.

There are currently around 4,900 environmental conservation organisations in the UK. There is an increasing requirement for highly skilled staff and a high demand for people with relevant practical experience. Competition for jobs in this sector, however, is high, and so it is really useful to gain some experience through voluntary work.

Job roles

Level 2 (Apprenticeship) jobs are:

- assistant conservation officer
- assistant ranger
- assistant warden
- dry stone waller
- estate worker
- field surveyor.

At Level 3 (Advanced Apprenticeship), positions are:

- access and recreation officer
- education and interpretation officer
- ranger/countryside officer
- specialist team leader (flood risk management)
- volunteer manager.

Work and training

On this Apprenticeship, you will discover more about environmental issues and how to promote a more sustainable environment. You will gain knowledge of habitat management and ecosystems and be aiming at a work-based qualification, delivered on the job, and an off-the-job technical certificate. You will need to take a one-day course in emergency first aid. On the Advanced Apprenticeship, you will also have to take an occupational test relevant to your employment. These tests are required when operating specific pieces of machinery and include:

- chainsaw maintenance and operation
- driving with a trailer
- safe use of strimmers/brushcutters
- tractor driving.

Qualifications available at Level 2 are:

- Level 2 Diploma in Work-based Environmental Conservation; or
- Level 2 Certificate in Dry Stone Walling
- Level 2 Award in Business for the Environment and Land-based Sector; or
- Level 2 Certificate in Land-based Activities.

Qualifications at Level 3 are:

- Level 3 Diploma in Work-based Environmental Conservation; or
- Level 3 Certificate in Dry Stone Walling
- Level 3 Award in Business Management for the Environment and Land-based sector; or
- Level 3 Award in Principles of Developing Environment and Land-based projects.

As an apprentice, you'll choose between a number of pathways:

- access and recreation
- environmental conservation
- rivers, coasts and waterways.

On the Advanced Apprenticeship, there is a further pathway in flood risk management. Alternatively you may choose to specialise in dry stone walling from the outset. The nature of the work will depend on your employer and the route you choose.

As an assistant conservation officer, you could be supporting work to protect, manage and enhance environments such as woodlands, grassland, wetland, moorland and possibly marine habitats. As a field surveyor, you would learn how to conduct surveys of natural habitats in order to identify, record and monitor the plant and animal species present. As a dry stone waller, you would rebuild, repair and maintain the many miles of wall found around the countryside.

On the Advanced Apprenticeship, you'll learn how to use good environmental practice at work and organise environmental projects. As a ranger, your role would be to encourage visitors to explore the countryside, promote awareness of the natural environment and protect the land for future enjoyment. As a volunteer manager, you could be responsible for recruiting, training, organising and supporting volunteers on environmental projects.

Entry requirements

There are no set entry requirements for the Apprenticeship programme. However you will be assessed to make sure you're able to achieve the outcomes of the programme. For an Advanced Apprenticeship, you'll need to hold the Level 2 Diploma in Work-based Environmental Conservation, the Level 2 Certificate in Dry Stone Walling or an equivalent qualification.

It is important to have an interest in the environment, sustainability and biodiversity and a positive attitude towards learning. It also helps if you are practical, enjoy solving problems and like working outdoors.

Salary once qualified

Depending on your role, you could earn between £10,000 and £18,000.

Progression

With experience and qualifications, it is possible to progress into management positions. It may also be possible to specialise in key conservation areas or move into environmental policy.

With an Advanced Apprenticeship, you could progress to further and higher education programmes such as an NVQ Level 4 in conservation management or a relevant Foundation degree, or to continue your development through industry training.

Floristry

Floristry is about designing, creating, selling and delivering floral displays. The industry is generally made up of small businesses, which are often linked together by larger organisations such as Interflora and Teleflorist. As an apprentice, you could be providing flowers for a variety of events, from weddings and funerals to conferences and state occasions. As businesses are small, you are also likely to be involved in other aspects of their running such as sales, marketing, accounts and stock ordering.

There are around 8,400 floristry businesses in the UK. Floristry is a competitive and growing industry.

Job roles

At Level 2 (Apprenticeship), roles are as follows:

- assistant florist
- florist
- flower cutter/conditioner.

Level 3 (Advanced Apprenticeship) positions are:

- buyer
- senior florist/floral designer supervisor
- tutor/assessor.

Work and training

On this Apprenticeship, you will learn how to produce imaginative floral arrangements for customers as well as developing your customer service and business skills. You will learn about plant care and maintenance and progress towards a work-based diploma, normally delivered on the job.

As an assistant florist, you would be helping the florist with flower arrangements and preparing plants and material for distribution. You would also help in the shop with customer service, transactions and taking orders. As a flower cutter, you could be preparing cut plant material before its arrangement to ensure that flowers and foliage last for the maximum time. As an apprentice at Level 2, you would take the Level 2 Diploma in Work-based Floristry.

As a senior florist or floral designer, you could be assembling and constructing diverse floral designs, for occasions from weddings to funerals. As a buyer, you would be responsible for selecting a range of plants and flowers to sell in florists. As a supervisor, you would be responsible for the day-to-day management of the shop, including staff and stock control. On the Advanced Apprenticeship, you would take the Level 3 Diploma in Work-based Floristry.

Entry requirements

There are no set entry requirements for the Apprenticeship. However, you will be assessed before starting the programme to make sure you're able to complete it. For the Advanced Apprenticeship, you will need to hold the Level 2 Diploma in Work-based Floristry or equivalent qualification.

It is important to have a flair for design and creativity and an interest in plants and flowers. It also helps if you have good communication skills and are reliable and self-motivated.

Salary once qualified

You may earn between £10,000 and £20,000 depending on your role.

Progression

There are good opportunities to progress into management roles. Florists with the necessary business skills sometimes start their own business and become self-employed.

With an Advanced Apprenticeship, you could progress to further or higher education programmes such as an NVQ Level 4 or a Foundation degree, or develop your career through relevant industry training.

Horticulture

Horticulture is a major UK industry offering a huge range of opportunities. This apprenticeship covers two parts of the horticulture industry: landscaping and production horticulture. Landscaping deals with the design, creation and maintenance of both rural and urban design landscapes. Production horticulture involves the large-scale growing and selling of plants, either as food products or as plants for gardening.

Landscaping offers opportunities in areas such as hard, soft and interior landscaping, sports turf and golf greenkeeping, public parks and green spaces, heritage gardens and private estates. As an apprentice, you could be working for a small contractor providing landscape gardening services or for a large multinational company on a motorway landscape project.

Apprentices in production horticulture might work for a small private nursery, a garden centre or a very large specialist farm. Businesses typically produce fruit, vegetables, plants, mushrooms, flowers, bulbs and trees.

Job roles

Level 2 (Apprenticeship) roles are:

- cemetery worker
- gardener
- greenkeeper/groundsperson
- interior landscaper
- packer
- skilled fruit production worker
- skilled intensive vegetable production worker
- skilled plant nursery worker/skilled horticulture worker
- skilled plant propagator
- tractor/machine operator.

At Level 3 (Advanced Apprenticeship), positions are:

- deputy head greenkeeper/groundsperson
- garden designer
- interior landscape designer
- parks officer
- team leader/gardener.

Work and training

In the Apprenticeship you will develop knowledge of plants and how to look after them, together with lots of practical skills. You may also learn business management skills such as sales, customer care and marketing. You will take a work-based diploma, delivered both on and off the job. You will also need to take a one-day course in emergency first aid, as well as an occupational test relevant to your employment. To complete the Advanced Apprenticeship, you will have to take an additional occupational test. These tests are required to ensure safety when operating specific pieces of machinery or using pesticides. Tests include those in:

- safe use of pesticides
- chainsaw and related operations
- forklift truck operations
- tractor driving
- ride-on mowers

- ladder safety/working at heights
- safe use of hedge trimmers
- safe operation of dumper trucks
- indoor plants.

As an apprentice you'll choose between the following pathways.

- Gardens and green space
- Horticulture
- Landscaping and parks
- Production horticulture
- Sports turf.

The nature of the work depends on your employer and the pathway you choose.

In production horticulture, you could be working in large glasshouses growing salad crops or be planting, tending, harvesting and storing all types of vegetables. As a greenkeeper, you would be ensuring grass is in peak condition for sports such as football, cricket or tennis. As an interior landscaper, you would learn how to design and install indoor planting schemes in, for example, shopping centres. As an apprentice gardener, you would assist the gardener with day-to-day tasks such as planting, pruning, weeding and mowing. At Level 2, you would be taking the Level 2 Diploma in Work-based Horticulture.

On the Advanced Apprenticeship, you could move into a supervisory role, for example leading a team of gardeners or greenkeepers. Or you may choose to specialise, for example in garden design, providing a complete garden design service, producing planting plans and including hard landscape elements such as paving and decking. On the Advanced Apprenticeship, you would be taking the Level 3 Diploma in Work-based Horticulture.

Entry requirements

There are no set entry requirements for an Apprenticeship. However, you will be assessed before starting the programme to make sure you're able to complete it successfully. For an Advanced Apprenticeship, you will need to hold the Level 2 Diploma in Work-based Horticulture or an equivalent qualification, or have sufficient practical experience.

It is important that you enjoy working with plants and care about the environment. It also helps if you are practical and enjoy solving problems. Employers in the landscaping industry may also look for an interest in design and creative skills.

Salary once qualified

You could earn between £10,000 and £15,000, depending on the role.

Progression

With experience and qualifications, there are opportunities to move into management roles in all areas of the horticulture industry, particularly production horticulture. There are also good opportunities for self-employment, for example as a gardener or a garden designer.

With an Advanced Apprenticeship, you could progress to further and higher education programmes such as an NVQ Level 4 or a Foundation degree, or develop your career by taking additional technical courses and professional qualifications in horticulture.

HEALTH, PUBLIC SERVICES AND CARE

Public services are all those that keep society going, from education and fire services to health care and social services, and help make our society a better place. There is a huge range of career opportunities in the field of health, public services and care, as this umbrella heading covers a diverse range of sectors, such as:

- community work
- education
- health care
- housing
- security services
- social care
- youth work.

As an apprentice in the health care sector, for example, you could be training to become a pharmacy technician or a dental nurse, and be working in the NHS or for a private organisation. In the social care sector you could be a care worker helping to meet the needs of the most vulnerable groups in our society, such as elderly people and those with special needs. Alternatively, you could choose to work with children in a range of settings from nurseries to children's centres. In other sectors you could train towards becoming a youth worker, probation services officer, security guard, community development worker or housing advice worker, for example.

Working environments and the skills you need vary widely. In many of the areas, you'll find your role involves offering support to people. This could be individuals who are moving from homelessness into their own accommodation or older people needing support to stay independent in their own homes. In these roles, your people skills and caring attitude will be important. In others, such as pharmacy technician, you will need technical and scientific knowledge.

You may be interested in a role in these sectors if you:

- enjoy working with people
- like the opportunity to help people
- want to make a difference to the society we live in
- enjoy working in a team
- enjoy learning practical skills
- like science and technical subjects (for certain roles).

Apprenticeships are available in the following sectors.

- Advice and guidance
- Children's care, learning and development
- Community development
- Community justice

- Dental nursing
- Emergency fire service operations
- Health and social care
- Housing
- Information and library services
- Optical science
- Pharmacy
- Security services
- Security systems
- Supporting teaching and learning in schools
- Youth work.

For information on the relevant Sector Skills Councils, which industries and apprenticeships they represent and important web addresses where you can find out more about apprenticeships and careers in this sector refer to Chapter 9.

Children's care, learning and development

This apprenticeship covers a range of opportunities for working with children (from birth to 16 years old), in settings or services whose main purpose is children's care, learning and development. As an apprentice, you could be working in a wide range of early learning and childcare settings, such as day nurseries, nursery schools and primary schools, pre-schools, crèches, out-of-school environments and children's centres or community programmes.

As more parents go out to work, there is a growing demand for trained childcare providers. As a result, the early years and childcare sector is expanding rapidly.

Job roles

At Level 2 (Apprenticeship), roles are:

- assistant playworker
- nursery assistant
- pre-school assistant.

Level 3 (Advanced Apprenticeship) positions are:

- childminder
- nursery nurse/early years practitioner
- pre-school leader
- senior playworker.

Work and training

As an apprentice, you will learn the skills and knowledge to work with children, gain an understanding of their development and put into practice the childcare theory you learn. You will work towards qualifications both on and off the job.

Qualifications available at Level 2 are:

- Level 2 NVQ in Children's Care, Learning and Development
- Level 2 Certificate for the Children and Young People's Workforce.

Qualifications at Level 3 are:

- Level 3 NVQ in Children's Care, Learning and Development
- Level 3 Diploma for the Children and Young People's Workforce.

On the Level 2 Apprenticeship, you will work under supervision as an assistant in an early learning or childcare setting. As a nursery assistant or pre-school assistant, you could be helping children develop and learn through activities such as play, counting games, storytelling and outings. You would encourage children to develop language, number and social skills. Your work would also involve observing and assessing children and producing reports on their development. In a day nursery, you could also be responsible for caring for babies, including feeding and dressing. You will look after the welfare of children and ensure that they are safe and well cared for.

On the Level 3 Advanced Apprenticeship, you will learn how to develop and promote positive relationships, promote children's development and maintain a healthy safe and secure environment and protect and promote children's rights. You will take on more of a supervisory or specialised role, for example working as a nursery nurse or childminder, and be responsible for a group of children. You would be working on your own initiative, planning and organising your own work and/or supervising assistants. As a childminder, you would be self-employed and usually care for children in your own home. Your role would be to provide plenty of fun and learning opportunities in a safe environment.

Entry requirements

There are no set entry requirements, but it is an advantage to have some GCSEs (A*–C), particularly in English and maths.

You will need to enjoy working with young children and have an interest in helping them learn and develop. It also helps if you are patient and caring and have good communication skills. For the Advanced Apprenticeship, you will need good planning and organisational skills.

Progression

Once you've gained a Level 3 qualification, there's considerable scope for progression. You could move up into more senior positions, such as team leader, deputy nursery manager, manager or officer in charge. You could take more qualifications and training, such as NVQ Level 4 in Children's Care, Learning and Development, a Level 4 Higher Professional Diploma in Early Years or leadership and management training.

You could also take a Foundation Degree in Early Years, which could lead on to an Honours degree. Once students have successfully completed their degree they can choose to work towards Early Years Professional (EYP) status. As an EYP, you could lead work with children, for example in a children's centre or full day care setting.

With the right qualifications and experience, you could set up your own private day nursery. There are also opportunities to work abroad, in large hotels and holiday centres and on cruise ships.

Community justice

This is an Advanced Apprenticeship, on which you will be supporting vulnerable people and developing skills to build safer communities. Work in community justice covers:

- prevention of offending and re-offending
- supervision of offenders in the community
- community-based rehabilitation projects.

The justice sector is a growing one, with a diverse range of opportunities. There are just over 50,000 employees in community justice-related initiatives. As an apprentice, you could be working in a wide range of settings and services, including for example probation or drug and alcohol services. You could be working for a local authority or a voluntary sector organisation.

Job roles

In this sector, you could work as:

- arrest referral worker
- community safety project worker
- prison substance misuse worker
- probation services officer
- voluntary sector project worker
- youth offending team (YOT) worker.

Work and training

On this Advanced Apprenticeship, you will work on the job towards the Level 3 NVQ in Community Justice and off the job at college towards the Level 3 Certificate in Community Justice. Depending on your job role, you will choose one of the following pathways:

- community safety
- working in drug and alcohol services
- working with offending behaviour
- youth justice.

There are also optional routes in working with victims, survivors and witnesses.

As an apprentice in drug and alcohol services, you would learn how to assess the needs of people with drug and alcohol problems and develop and implement care plans. You may also receive training in carrying out drug screening tests as part of a drug treatment programme. Your work could involve helping people move on with their lives by supporting them into employment, training or education.

In youth justice services, you would be working in partnership with other agencies such as the police and social services to reduce the offending behaviour of children and young people. Your work could involve mentoring, organising activities and offering counselling and support. You may also be supervising sentences served in the community by children and young people.

As an apprentice in the probation service, your role would involve working with individuals or groups of offenders on a wide range of programmes aimed at reducing offending behaviour. You will also be promoting the rehabilitation of offenders and helping them reintegrate into the community.

In community safety service, your role would focus on reducing crime and disorder and making the community you work in a safer place to live. Working in partnership with police and local voluntary organisations you would help tackle issues such as crime and antisocial behaviour, drugs prevention, domestic abuse, housing, employment and regeneration.

Entry requirements

There are no set pre-entry requirements. You will, however, need to demonstrate that you are able to achieve all of the required outcomes of the Advanced Apprenticeship. You will have to complete a Criminal Records Bureau check at an enhanced level. Depending on your job role, other security checks may also be required.

Above all, you will need to be enthusiastic about working with your particular service users. You will also need to be responsible, open-minded and able to communicate well with all types of people from different backgrounds.

Salary once qualified

After completing the Advanced Apprenticeship, you could earn from £18,000 to £20,000.

Progression

The Advanced Apprenticeship in Community Justice provides an entry-level qualification for young people who want to start a career in the justice sector or substance misuse field. You will gain the skills and knowledge to apply for jobs such as community safety officer, substance misuse practitioner, trainee probation officer or YOT worker. Progression in this sector could be to senior practitioner status or a management position. You could also take a relevant higher education course, for example the Diploma in Probation Studies or the Professional Certificate in Youth Justice.

Dental nursing

On this Advanced Apprenticeship, you will be supporting the dentist and other members of the dental team in patient care. You could be working in a dental practice, a hospital, the community or a specialist dental hospital.

There are over 44,000 dental nurses registered with the General Dental Council (GDC) and the majority are employed in general dental practices. There is a shortage of qualified dental nurses in many areas.

Job role
Dental nurse is the sole job role under the Advanced Apprenticeship.

Work and training
You will gain a solid foundation in both knowledge and the practical skills needed to succeed in this career area. You will work on the job towards the Level 3 NVQ in Dental Nursing and off the job towards the Level 3 Award in Dental Nursing. All dental nurses must be registered with the GDC and licensed to practice. This Advanced Apprenticeship will prepare you for qualification on completion of the course.

You will learn how to contribute to the safe and effective care of patients by:

- promoting and maintaining health and safety in the workplace
- ensuring a high standard of infection control in the clinical environment
- providing chair-side and patient support.

As a dental nursing apprentice, you will learn how to carry out a range of duties, including patient care, sterilising equipment, preparing the dental room and equipment and taking notes during examination. You would also help with reception work.

Entry requirements
There are no set entry requirements. Some employers have their own qualification requirements and may want candidates to have four GCSEs (grade A*–D) or equivalent, including English at Grade A*–C and three others, preferably including maths and a science.

It is important to have good people skills so you can make patients feel at ease and communicate with colleagues. You should also have a keen interest in dentistry.

Salary once qualified
Dental nurses can earn from £15,000 to £17,000 once qualified.

Progression
On successful completion of this Advanced Apprenticeship, you will be able to register with the GDC and go straight into employment in a variety of dental settings including private practices, orthodontists or hospitals. You may also choose to progress to further learning in higher education, for example.

There are many opportunities for well-qualified dental nurses to progress in the sector in dental therapy, hygiene, oral health promotion or dental practice management. You could also move on to related health care roles in nursing or radiography.

Health and social care

This apprenticeship covers a wide range of roles in the health and social care sectors. As an apprentice, you could be working for the NHS, an independent care provider, a local authority or a voluntary organisation. In the health care sector, you could be working in hospitals, the community, hospices, private clinics or doctors' surgeries, while in social care you might work in a residential care home, day care centre or in a client's own home.

The health and social care sectors are both large, with jobs available throughout the UK. There are around 1.7 million people working in health care in England alone, and the social care sector is rapidly expanding because people are living longer and also looking to be more independent and stay in their own homes wherever possible.

Job roles in social care

Level 2 (Apprenticeship) roles are:

- care assistant
- community support worker
- day care assistant
- home care worker
- personal care assistant.

At Level 3 (Advanced Apprenticeship), you could be a:

- care manager
- day care officer
- senior home care worker
- senior support worker.

Job roles in health care

Roles at Level 2 (Apprenticeship) are:

- health care assistant
- health care support worker
- nursing assistant
- support service workers (cleaner, porter, laundry assistant, catering assistant).

Level 3 (Advanced Apprenticeship) positions are:

- dietetic assistant
- donor carer
- maternity/midwifery support worker
- occupational therapy or physiotherapy assistant
- radiotherapy assistant
- senior health care assistant
- speech and language therapy assistant.

Work and training

As an apprentice in health and social care, you will work towards qualifications both on and off the job. On this apprenticeship, there are various pathways at both Level 2 and Level 3, and the qualifications you take will depend on your role.

Qualifications at Level 2 are:

- Level 2 NVQ in Health and Social Care; or
- Level 2 NVQ in Health; or
- Level 2 NVQ in Support Services in Health Care; and
- Level 2 Certificate in Health and Social Care.

At Level 3, qualifications are:

- Level 3 NVQ in Health and Social Care; or
- Level 3 NVQ in Health; and
- Level 3 Certificate in Health and Social Care; or
- Level 3 Certificate in Working in the Health Sector.

As an apprentice in health care, you could be working in support services, making and changing beds, serving food to patients or moving patients between different wards. Alternatively, you could be supporting doctors and nurses in clinical roles. As a nursing assistant, for example, you would be working under the guidance of qualified nurses to provide basic patient care.

On the Advanced Apprenticeship, you could choose to specialise in a particular area. You could be working, for example, as a donor carer collecting and testing blood samples and looking after blood donors, or working as an assistant to various health care professionals such as occupational therapists or speech and language therapists.

As an apprentice in social care, you will be supporting people with particular needs, such as those with mental health issues, learning or physical disabilities or the elderly. As a care assistant in a residential home, you would get to know residents and provide support with essential everyday activities such as washing, dressing, making breakfast and doing exercises. As a home care worker, you would visit people with additional needs in their homes. Your role would be to provide personal care and practical support such as helping with the laundry, cleaning and food preparation. You would help people to stay living at home with as much independence as possible.

On the Advanced Apprenticeship, you will take on more responsibilities. At supervisory level you will also cover care planning, medication and supporting junior staff.

Entry requirements

There are no minimum entry requirements for the Apprenticeship, but a Level 2 qualification in health and social care is necessary for the Advanced Apprenticeship.

It is important to have good communication and interpersonal skills and respect for patients or service users. It also helps if you are patient, calm in new situations and interested in people. In some roles, you will need a suitable level of physical fitness to perform certain tasks, such as lifting and handling.

Progression

There are a wide range of opportunities to progress in the health and social care sector. After completing the Advanced Apprenticeship you could progress to NVQ Level 4 in Health and Social Care, or to higher education in subjects such as midwifery, nursing or social care.

Organisations such as the NHS have clearly defined career structures, and employees are encouraged to take additional training and work towards promotion. Many social care employers also have a defined career structure and it is possible to move into roles as a team leader, deputy manager or manager, or even to become a director of care.

Housing

This apprenticeship covers a range of opportunities in the housing sector, essentially in 'social housing' – i.e. houses and flats rented from local authorities, housing associations or other similar not-for-profit organisations.

Increasingly, housing is about neighbourhoods and making sure that they are decent places to live. Housing associations are often involved in regeneration projects, for example on poor estates, improving the area so people can take pride in their community. Housing is also about helping people in need, whether they are on a low income, have special requirements, and includes older people and those with disabilities or drug and alcohol problems.

As an apprentice in housing, you will help to make people's lives better. You could be working in the public, voluntary or private rented sector.

Job roles

At Level 2 (Apprenticeship), roles comprise:

- housing administration assistant
- housing assistant
- housing customer service assistant.

Level 3 (Advanced Apprenticeship) positions are:

- allocations officer
- community development officer
- customer services officer
- housing advice worker
- housing officer
- hostel support worker
- maintenance officer

- outreach officer
- sheltered housing officer
- supported housing officer
- tenancy enforcement officer.

Work and training

On the Apprenticeship and Advanced Apprenticeship you will work both on and off the job towards the following nationally- and industry-recognised qualifications.

At Level 2, you'll take:

- Level 2 NVQ in Housing; and
- Level 2 Certificate in Housing; or
- Level 2 Certificate in Housing Maintenance.

Qualifications at Level 3, meanwhile, are:

- Level 3 NVQ in Housing; and
- Level 3 Certificate in Housing; or
- Level 3 Certificate in Housing Maintenance.

On this apprenticeship you'll learn about customer services, housing management, lettings and allocations, supported housing (which covers shared housing, hostels and sheltered housing), housing advice, homelessness and repairs and maintenance.

As a housing apprentice, your role will depend on your employer and which sector you're working in. As a housing assistant, you could be working in the housing department of a local authority, for example, inspecting housing for repairs, collecting rents or working with tenants to find out what housing benefits they are entitled to. You would liaise with a range of organisations, from community groups to the police and social services.

You might be working in an advice centre, giving advice and guidance to people who are experiencing housing difficulties. They may be homeless, unable to pay their mortgage or rent, wanting repairs or be in a dispute with their landlord or neighbours. Your role would involve interviewing people to assess their problems and help them to find solutions. Your work would also include referring people to other support services, for example social workers and housing officers.

You could be working for a charity as a project worker in a homeless hostel, supporting people living in temporary accommodation. Your role would involve advising people on welfare benefits, housing and training and employment opportunities. You would also provide support and advice to help them prepare for living independently. You could be working with vulnerable adults, including people with mental health issues and drug or alcohol problems.

Entry requirements

There are no specific entry requirements as employers set their own entry criteria. Some may expect a good selection of GCSEs (at grades A*–C).

It helps to have good communication, negotiation and problem-solving skills. It would also be useful if you have an understanding of different cultures and backgrounds and the ability to deal tactfully with difficult situations.

Salary once qualified

You could earn £14,000 to £20,000 depending on the role.

Progression

There are good opportunities to progress from assistant-level roles to housing officer then to housing manager or team leader, and on to more senior roles such as senior or area housing manager, and even housing director.

There are also opportunities to specialise in certain areas, such as housing for people with special needs or the elderly.

After the Advanced Apprenticeship, you could develop your career by taking higher-level qualifications such as the NVQ Level 4 in Housing, a Foundation Degree in Housing or the Chartered Institute of Housing (CIH)'s qualifications at Level 4. There are also degrees and postgraduate diplomas relating to housing.

HOSPITALITY, LEISURE, TRAVEL AND TOURISM

The hospitality, leisure, travel and tourism sector is one of the UK's largest employers with almost two million people, which equates to seven per cent of all UK jobs. This sector offers a wide diversity of career opportunities across a range of industries, from travel and tourism to hospitality and catering. This section also covers the active leisure and learning sector, which offers a variety of opportunities in sport, recreation and health and fitness.

Working environments in these sectors vary widely. You could be working for a high street travel agency or an airline, for a local leisure centre or a professional football club, in a theme park or on a cruise ship, or for a restaurant chain or five-star hotel.

The skills and abilities you need will vary according to the role and industry you are working in. If you have good communication skills, a friendly personality and enjoy working in a team, you may be interested in one of the many customer-facing roles available. You could train, for example, to become an air cabin crew member, travel consultant, waiter, bar person or receptionist. If you prefer to be behind the scenes, you could train to become a chef, kitchen assistant or housekeeper.

If you enjoy physical activity and like working with people, you could become a coach, fitness instructor or activity leader. If you have a sporting talent you could focus on your sporting career while studying for a qualification at the same time. In other roles, such as sports centre management, you will need good management and organisational skills.

There are also good opportunities in these sectors to travel and work abroad.

You may be interested in a role in these sectors if you:

- enjoy working with people
- enjoy working in a team
- like the opportunity to give excellent customer service
- have an interest in travel and tourism, hospitality and catering, or in sport and leisure.

Also, depending on the role, you might:

- enjoy learning practical skills
- like motivating people
- like organising people or things
- enjoy sports, physical activity and exercise
- have a passion for travel
- are excited by food and cooking.

Apprenticeships in these sectors are available in the following areas.

- Active leisure and learning
- Cabin crew

- Hospitality and catering
- Sporting excellence
- Travel services

For information on the relevant Sector Skills Councils, which industries and apprenticeships they represent and important web addresses where you can find out more, refer to Chapter 9.

Active leisure and learning

This apprenticeship includes pathways in many aspects of sport and leisure, from coaching to exercise instruction to playwork. On this apprenticeship, you could be working in leisure centres, gyms, swimming pools, stadiums and private sports clubs, as well as at outdoor activity centres and adventure playgrounds.

The active leisure and learning industry is a large sector, directly employing an estimated 620,000 people in the UK, plus in excess of 5.8 million volunteers.

Job roles

Active leisure and learning roles are as follows:

- activity holiday organiser
- activity leader
- event security
- fitness instructor
- ground safety officer
- health and fitness centre attendant
- leisure and sports manager
- leisure and theme park attendant
- outdoor centre attendant
- play centre attendant
- play leader
- sport and leisure centre assistant
- sports coach, instructor or official
- sports player
- spectator control
- steward and related occupations
- youth and community workers.

Work and training

On both the Apprenticeship and Advanced Apprenticeship, you will be working on the job towards a relevant NVQ and off the job towards an appropriate technical certificate. The qualifications you take will depend on the role you are working in and the pathway you choose.

The Apprenticeship covers Level 2 qualifications for the following pathways.

- Activity leadership
- Coaching
- Fitness instructing
- Leisure centre operations
- Playwork
- Spectator safety.

The Advanced Apprenticeship covers Level 3 qualifications for the following pathways.

- Coaching
- Instructing physical activity and exercise
- Leisure management
- Outdoor programmes
- Playwork
- Sports development

On the Apprenticeship, you could be employed across a range of jobs such as leisure centre assistant, activity leader, fitness instructor, play leader or coach. You will be working at an operational level, whereas on the Advanced Apprenticeship you will be working higher up in roles such as supervisor, senior coach or instructor, duty manager or team leader.

Opportunities under this apprenticeship are very broad. If you enjoy working with people, you could teach swimming, lead outdoor activity trips or help gym users achieve their fitness goals. You would learn how to motivate and instruct a broad range of people and be using and developing your communication skills.

This apprenticeship is not just for people who enjoy sports. If you have good management and organisational skills, you could help run a sport and leisure centre both behind the scenes and front of house. Alternatively, if you enjoy attending sports events then you could train in spectator safety or stewarding and work at large events, festivals or local matches.

Entry requirements

There are no set entry requirements for the Apprenticeship. However, you will need to demonstrate that you have the potential to complete the programme as well as being numerate and literate and able to communicate well with a range of people. If you are going to be working with children or vulnerable adults, you will need to undergo a Criminal Records Bureau check.

To work in this industry, it also helps if you are proactive, confident, motivated, independent and customer-focused.

You will need a relevant qualification at Level 2 or to have completed the Level 2 Apprenticeship before moving on to the Advanced Apprenticeship.

Salary once qualified

On qualification, you could earn £12,000 to £18,000 depending on your role.

Progression

From the Apprenticeship, you could progress to the Advanced Apprenticeship, into a wide range of operational jobs in the sector or on to further education. From the Advanced

Apprenticeship, you could move into a wide range of jobs in supervisory roles or on to a higher education course such as a Foundation degree. You could also advance your career by taking NVQs at Level 4 and move into higher-level roles such as leisure centre manager or regional or national coach.

Cabin crew

This Apprenticeship is for people who want to become an air cabin crew member. You could be working for a large airline flying to many international destinations or for a small carrier operating flights in the UK. Your role would be to ensure that passengers are safe and comfortable for the duration of their flight.

Airlines provide budget, long-haul, short-haul, scheduled and chartered flights to both UK and international destinations. Global events and international politics can significantly affect the volume of passengers choosing air travel; for example, terrorist attacks can have a major impact on aviation.

Job roles

Roles on this Apprenticeship are:

- air cabin crew member
- flight attendant.

Work and training

On this Apprenticeship, you will work on the job towards NVQ Level 2 in Aviation Operations in the Air – Cabin Crew, and off the job towards a relevant technical certificate at Level 2.

You'll learn how to prepare the inside of the aircraft for a flight by checking supplies and making sure the right safety equipment is in place. You'll also ensure the aircraft is clean and tidy. You'll welcome passengers on board, help them find their seats and demonstrate emergency equipment and procedures.

During the flight, you could be serving food and drink, selling duty-free goods and making general in-flight announcements. Cabin crew are also responsible for dealing with any problems during the flight, from someone feeling ill to somebody causing a disturbance. After landing, your duties could include ensuring that passengers disembark safely from the aircraft and tidying the galley.

In this role, you will be responsible for the safety and care of airline passengers, including during emergency situations when cabin crew need to ensure that passengers follow procedure and use safety equipment correctly. As an apprentice, you will therefore be trained to deal with a wide range of security and emergency situations. You might also learn about areas such as immigration regulations, cultural awareness and how to complete flight reports and other paperwork.

Entry requirements

Cabin crew apprentices must:

- be over 18 years old
- measure between 5' 2" and 6' 5" tall, with weight in proportion to height
- have a good standard of general education – most airlines require four to five GCSEs (A*–C) or equivalent including English language and mathematics
- have normal colour vision and good eyesight
- be physically fit and able to swim approximately 25 metres
- be able to provide full information about your background to obtain an air-side security pass.

The physical requirements set reflect the critical role of cabin crew in ensuring the safety and well-being of passengers in emergency situations.

As a member of a cabin crew, you will be working with customers, other team members and colleagues at a range of airports. It therefore helps if you have excellent communication skills, a friendly personality, a calm and reassuring manner and a smart appearance. As cabin crew members are the 'face' of an airline, you'll need to understand the importance of good customer service.

Salary once qualified

You could earn between £12,000 and £16,000 on qualification.

Progression

On completion of the Cabin Crew Apprenticeship at Level 2, successful apprentices will be able to work as air cabin crew. They may choose to progress to supervisory roles such as purser or senior cabin crew or take the NVQ Level 3 in Aviation Operations in the Air – Cabin Crew.

Cabin crew frequently move on to roles elsewhere in an airline's organisational structure, for example in rostering, training and recruitment, sales and marketing.

Further progression from a senior cabin crew role could lead to a general management position at an airline and a Foundation Degree in Leadership and Management.

Hospitality and catering

This apprenticeship covers a range of occupations in the hospitality and catering industry, which is about providing for the public in various ways from serving food and drink to offering accommodation. On this apprenticeship, you could be working for a luxury five-star hotel, a national restaurant chain, a fast food franchise, a local contract catering company or a school canteen.

The hospitality and catering industry is large and diverse, offering a range of opportunities. Employers include:

- hotels and guest houses
- restaurants, cafes and fast food outlets
- pubs, clubs and bars
- theme parks, museums, art galleries and leisure resorts
- contract caterers
- schools, colleges, hospitals and nursing homes
- railway, airport and cruise ship companies.

There is lots of choice in this industry; you could even work overseas once you've qualified or you could start your own business.

Job roles

Level 2 (Apprenticeship) roles are:

- barperson, cellarperson and possibly bar supervisor
- cook, school cook, team member or chef
- craft chef
- kitchen/catering assistant or team member
- housekeeper
- receptionist
- team member/supervisor in a holiday park or small hotel
- waiter or silver service waiter
- youth hostel worker/supervisor.

At Level 3 (Advanced Apprenticeship), roles are:

- head of reception or front-of-house supervisor
- head housekeeper
- sous chef or team supervisor
- unit manager in a contract catering company
- unit manager in a hotel chain
- unit or regional supervisor/manager in a restaurant/pub chain with multiple outlets.

Work and training

On the Apprenticeship, you will work towards a relevant NVQ Diploma at Level 2 and a Level 2 technical certificate. On the Advanced Apprenticeship, you will work towards a relevant NVQ diploma and a technical certificate, both at Level 3. These qualifications may be integrated into an organisation's in-house training scheme, with apprentices learning in their own time, possibly through online training.

On the Apprenticeship at Level 2, you are likely to start in an assistant role. This could be a customer-facing position such as a waiter, barperson or receptionist, or you might prefer to be behind the scenes in a role such as housekeeper or kitchen assistant.

You'll choose one of a number of the following career pathways.

- Drinks service
- Food and drink service
- Food production and cooking
- Front office
- Hospitality services
- Housekeeping
- Kitchen services
- Professional cookery.

If you're interested in service, you could train on the food and drink service pathway as a waiter and learn how to serve customers or as a barperson in drinks service. The kitchen services pathway is suitable for people working in commercial kitchens such as branded high street restaurants.

The professional cookery pathway is for those who want to train as chefs. You will learn the classic way of preparing culinary dishes and gain a greater knowledge of preparation and cooking techniques suitable for professional catering in hotels, restaurants and pubs. On this pathway there are new options at Level 2 to specialise in Asian or Oriental cuisine. On the food production and cooking pathway, meanwhile, you would learn how to cook on a large scale for organisations such as schools or the NHS.

If you are interested in working in the field of reception, you could choose the front office pathway. The hospitality services pathway is for jobs in smaller places, such as running a B&B or youth hostel, while the housekeeping pathway is focused on making sure the accommodation is kept beautiful and clean.

On the Advanced Apprenticeship, you can choose either the professional cookery pathway or the hospitality supervision pathway. This Level 3 Apprenticeship is specifically for those working in a supervisory capacity in areas such as bars, restaurants, banqueting, accommodation, front of house, catering and so on. You will be supervising staff, organising resources, ensuring health, safety and hygiene, preparing food and dealing with customers' problems.

Entry requirements

There are no specific entry requirements for the Apprenticeship, although employers may set their own criteria and you will need to assure them you are capable of completing the programme. For entry to the Advanced Apprenticeship, you will need to have successfully completed either the hospitality Apprenticeship, a hospitality-related qualification at Level 2 or have gained Level 2 vocational experience and skills.

You'll need good customer service, communication and team work skills. It also helps if you are enthusiastic and hard-working with a positive attitude.

Salary once qualified

After this apprenticeship, you could earn between £9,000 and £13,000 depending on your role.

Progression

On successful completion of the Apprenticeship, you can progress to the Advanced Apprenticeship. There are opportunities in all areas of hospitality and catering to progress to supervisory and management roles. As a bar supervisor, for example, you could become a bar manager, publican or regional manager and ultimately progress into general management. As a chef, you could progress to sous chef and then head chef or catering manager. There are also opportunities to become self-employed, for example by running your own restaurant or small hotel.

From the Advanced Apprenticeship, it is possible to progress into higher education, for example taking a Foundation degree in Culinary Arts or Hospitality Management, or on to other qualifications such as management NVQs at Levels 4 and 5.

Case Study

Robin Brisby

Robin is on an Advanced Apprenticeship in Hospitality and Catering: Professional Cookery route.

'I've always been interested in cooking. When I was younger, I used to help my grandma to make the Sunday dinner, and she taught me cake making too. When I was at school I had work experience waiting tables at a local pub that serves meals. I then got an evening and weekend job there pot washing.

'I left school after my GCSEs and took a course in professional cookery at Level 1, which was full-time for a year. During this time, I worked part-time pot washing and waiting tables at another pub, and the head chef asked if I'd like to start doing food preparation as well. I started on the salad bar and preparing vegetables, before slowly moving my way around the kitchen, preparing soups then meat and fish dishes. After I'd finished the professional cookery course, the head chef, who also owned the pub, offered me an Apprenticeship and I was really pleased.

'After finishing the Level 2 Apprenticeship I moved back to the pub I had first worked for. I'm now taking an Advanced Apprenticeship and working towards NVQ Level 3 in Professional Cookery and a technical certificate. I come into college one day a week and spend the rest of my time at work. I'm working as a sous chef alongside one other chef. I really enjoy all aspects of my work. I'm really glad I've taken the Apprenticeship route as I'm earning money, gaining work experience and meeting people from a wide range of backgrounds.

'I'd like to stay with this pub after my apprenticeship, as it is part of a company that owns a number of hotels, pubs and restaurants in this region. I'd like to get experience of different areas in hospitality, such as stock-taking or buying, and get a better understanding of how it all works. Ultimately, I'm very happy with what I'm doing and would be glad to stay in the kitchens as a sous chef. Basically, what I've done is taken my hobby a step further. I just like cooking!'

Sporting excellence

The Advanced Apprenticeship in sporting excellence is for young athletes and players (aged 16–18) who have the realistic potential to achieve excellence in their sport and are seeking to perform at the highest level as their main career goal. It is a structured national training and development route across many sports for talented young athletes, who may go on to represent their country at Olympic level or gain professional contracts.

There are currently more than 2,500 athletes on the programme throughout England.

Job roles

Positions on this programme are:

- apprentice at a professional sports club
- athlete in the 'academy environment' at a professional club
- elite athlete
- Talented Athlete Scholarship Scheme (TASS) athlete.

Work and training

This Advanced Apprenticeship doesn't simply teach you how to 'play the game' – it is designed to ensure that top young athletes receive the support and training they require to succeed in today's elite sporting environment. The programme has also been designed so that if an athlete falls short of their ultimate goal, they have the skills, knowledge and qualifications to follow a secondary or supplementary career.

You will have a greater number of quality coaching hours and will work, on the job, towards NVQ Level 3 in Achieving Excellence in Sport. You will learn about the technical, tactical, physical and psychological aspects of your chosen sport, and also address wider issues such as lifestyle, communication skills, health and safety and career management. You will work towards relevant technical certificates as well, which comprise 780 guided learning hours, chosen from a wide range of academic or vocational qualifications such as BTEC, AS and A levels. If you wanted, for example, to go to university after your Apprenticeship, you could choose sport-related A levels, or if you want to be a coach you might choose coaching qualifications.

The programme is currently operating across a diverse range of competitive sports including athletics, badminton, basketball, cricket, football, golf, judo, motor sports, netball, rugby, swimming, table tennis and tennis.

Entry requirements

Selection for this Advanced Aprenticeship is determined by your status in your chosen sport. To be eligible for selection you will need to be one of the following:

- a full-time contracted apprentice at a professional club
- a full-time elite athlete/player receiving support from the National Lottery World Class programme, and identified by the respective national governing body of your sport, such as UK Athletics

- involved in TASS
- involved in an 'academy environment' at a professional club but not yet offered-full time terms.

Salary once qualified

Starting salaries vary according to sport and ability.

Progression

The programme provides a number of progression routes. It prepares you for the working world and/or higher education – whether that is on the pitch, in an office, teaching others or competing on a world stage. You may be offered a professional contract, invitation on to a World Class Performance Programme or on a relevant tour. You may decide to progress to higher education – degrees are available in a range of sports-related subjects. Alternatively. there is a wide choice of either semi-professional and/or sport-related careers.

Travel services

This apprenticeship covers a range of travel services roles, from working as a leisure travel consultant to customer service advisor or resort representative. You could be working for a travel agent or tour operator, maybe in a high street travel agency, a contact centre or in a holiday resort overseas.

There are nearly 100,000 employees working for the travel services industry in the UK, working in 9,900 travel services enterprises. These range from small independent organisations to major retail travel agent chains with branches throughout the country.

Job roles

At Level 2 (Apprenticeship), you could be a:

- business travel consultant
- chalet worker
- customer service advisor
- leisure travel consultant
- resort representative
- tour guide
- travel advisor.

Level 3 (Advanced Apprenticeship) roles are:

- business travel consultant
- chalet worker
- leisure travel consultant
- resort representative
- senior customer service advisor
- senior travel advisor
- senior travel consultant

- team leader
- tour guide.

Work and training

On the Apprenticeship, you would work on the job towards a Level 2 NVQ Diploma in Travel Services and off the job towards a Level 2 Certificate in Travel Services. You would be working under supervision. On the Advanced Apprenticeship, you would work on the job towards a Level 3 NVQ Diploma in Travel Services and off the job towards a Level 3 Certificate in Travel Services. You would be in more of a supervisory role and responsible for planning you own work.

On both the Apprenticeship and Advanced Apprenticeship you can choose from the following pathways.

- Leisure and business
- Tour operators – head office
- Tour operators – field staff

All apprentices learn about worldwide travel and tourism destinations and principles of customer service in hospitality, leisure, travel and tourism.

The leisure and business route focuses on the largely customer-facing role of a travel agent. As a consultant for a travel agent, you'll learn a lot more than how to operate a computer and search for holidays. You will find out how to deliver effective customer service, communicate well with customers and suppliers and sort out any queries and problems. The role also requires a large amount of product knowledge. You could be arranging travel itineraries, costing products that your company offers or answering queries about travel destinations.

On the tour operators – head office route, you could be working in a call centre, helping customers make travel plans by checking availability and costs, making bookings and processing payments. The tour operators – field staff route is a specialist one, aimed at staff who deal with customers as part of their holiday experience. On this route, you would generally be based in a holiday resort overseas, working as a representative dealing with transfers and accommodation, or as a tour guide planning and delivering guided tours.

Entry requirements

There are no specific entry requirements for the Apprenticeship since employers set their own criteria. Candidates starting an Advanced Apprenticeship need to have either successfully completed the Travel Services Apprenticeship or have a travel services-related qualification at Level 2; or, they could have gained Level 2-comparable vocational experience and skills, for example by working in a relevant area for at least nine months to a year.

It is important that you have an interest in and enthusiasm for the travel services industry. It also helps if you can communicate well with a range of people, enjoy being part of a team, have organisational skills and are able to work to deadlines.

Salary once qualified

You could earn around £12,000 or upwards on completion of your apprenticeship.

Progression

Apprentices on the leisure and business route can progress into roles such as senior travel consultant, travel agency manager and eventually general management roles. Apprentices on the tour operators – head office route can progress to team leader, supervisory and managerial roles in an organisation. At larger employers, there are also opportunities to move out into the field, for example as overseas resort staff. Apprentices on the tour operators – field staff route can move on to roles such as resort manager or island/country manager.

There is a clear progression route from the Apprenticeship to the Advanced Apprenticeship. After completion of the Advanced Apprenticeship, there are opportunities to go on to management NVQs at Level 4 and 5 or into higher education, such as a Foundation degree in Travel. Apprentices on the field staff route can also choose to take specialist qualifications, such as language-based and guiding qualifications.

RETAIL AND COMMERCIAL ENTERPRISE

Retail and commercial enterprise covers a number of sectors and industries involved in providing goods and services, either for other businesses or directly to customers. There is a wide range of career opportunities in the retail sector, the logistics industry and in service industries such as hair, nail, beauty and spa, cleaning services, property services and mail services.

Retailers sell a vast range of products, from food and furniture to clothing and electrical equipment, and they rely on these being in the right place, in the right quantities and at the right time – as do many other businesses. This is known as logistics, and involves all kinds of transport from planes and trains to trucks and ships to move things around the UK and the rest of the world.

In the UK, there are:

- over 3 million people employed in retail
- around 2.3 million people employed in logistics
- around 450,000 people employed in cleaning
- over 240,000 people employed in hair and beauty.

As an apprentice in this sector, you could be working in a superstore or chain store, a specialist warehousing or freight company, a hair or beauty salon, a luxury hotel or cruise ship, a hospital or office building, an estate agents or a specialist mail service provider. You could train in a wide range of occupations including, for example, sales assistant or visual merchandiser, purchasing clerk or warehouse operative, nail or beauty therapist, domestic or industrial cleaner, estate agent or postal worker.

The skills you need will vary widely depending on the role and the industry you're working in. Many of the jobs in this sector, however, are customer-facing and focus on service. You may be interested in these jobs if you have good communication and people skills and can build good relationships. If you are also highly dexterous (i.e. good with your hands) and have an interest in science subjects, then you may be interested in a role in the hair and beauty industries.

If you enjoy practical, hands-on tasks, you may be suited to a job in cleaning services, where you could be cleaning streets, buildings or clothes, or in warehousing, where you could work as a forklift truck driver or operative. If you'd like to travel, you may be interested in a driving role in logistics.

For some roles, such as hairdressing and visual merchandising, a degree of artistic skill and flair is useful. In other roles, such as management, you will need leadership skills.

Number skills and good organisational skills are important in this sector. You will also need a good level of physical fitness for many jobs.

You may be interested in a role in this sector if you:

- have an interest in providing excellent customer service
- enjoy working with people
- enjoy working in a team
- have an interest in retail, logistics or service industries.

Also, depending on the role, you might:

- enjoy learning practical skills
- enjoy driving and travel
- enjoy science subjects
- like to be creative
- like motivating and leading people
- like organising people or things.

Apprenticeships are available in the following sectors.

- Barbering
- Beauty therapy
- Carry and deliver goods
- Cleaning and support services
- Driving goods vehicles
- Facilities management
- Hairdressing
- Logistics operations management
- Mail services
- Nail services
- Property services
- Purchasing and supply management
- Retail
- Spa therapy
- Traffic office
- Warehousing and storage.

Note: if you are interested in working in the service industries, you may also want to look at the Hospitality, Leisure, Travel and Tourism section above (page 116), which covers other service industries, and also Vehicles and Transport below (page 141), which covers the passenger transport sector.

For information on the relevant Sector Skills Councils, which industries and apprenticeships they represent and web addresses where you can find out more, refer to Chapter 9.

Beauty therapy

On this apprenticeship, you will learn how to use a range of facial and body treatments to make your clients look and feel better. You could be working in a variety of locations throughout the UK, including salons and beauty clinics, hospitals, care homes, spas, hotels and health clubs. There are also opportunities to work overseas, for example on board a cruise ship or in holiday destinations. Beauty therapists can also be self-employed.

In the UK, there are 4,800 beauty salons and 5,800 hairdressing salons that offer beauty therapy treatments. Many beauty therapy salons have more extensive provision, such as nail services and spa facilities.

Job roles

At Level 2 (Apprenticeship), roles comprise:

- junior beauty therapist
- skincare and make-up consultant.

Level 3 (Advanced Apprenticeship) positions are:

- beauty therapist
- electrolysist
- masseur
- make-up artist.

Work and training

On the Apprenticeship and Advanced Apprenticeship, you will work on the job towards a Level 2 NVQ Diploma in Beauty Therapy and Level 3 NVQ Diploma in Beauty Therapy respectively. There are career pathways in general beauty therapy and beauty therapy – make-up at Levels 2 and 3, and a further pathway in massage at Level 3.

On the Apprenticeship, you will assist senior therapists and learn how to carry out a range of treatments including applying make-up and tanning products, manicures and pedicures, waxing body hair, nail extensions, ear piercing and shaping and colouring brows.

On the Advanced Apprenticeship, you will work as a beauty therapist and learn further techniques such as head and body massage, Indian head massage and UV tanning treatments, as well as more complicated electronic treatments to improve facial and skin conditions or remove unwanted hair.

Entry requirements

There are no specific entry requirements for the Apprenticeship, although employers may set their own criteria and you will need to prove that you're capable of completing the programme.

It is an advantage to have had previous work experience in the beauty industry and have three GCSEs at grade D or above in English, maths, science or biology. For the Advanced Apprenticeship, you will need an NVQ Level 2 in Beauty Therapy or equivalent. It is an advantage to have previous work experience in the beauty industry and have four GCSEs at grade D or above in English, maths, science and biology.

You should have good practical, organisational and verbal communication skills, a high degree of dexterity and good hand–eye co-ordination. It helps to have patience, tolerance and a good sense of humour, as beauty therapists rely on repeat business from satisfied customers. You also need to take care of your own appearance and be presentable. You will need a high degree of physical stamina.

Salary once qualified

You could earn £12,000 to £17,000 after your apprenticeship.

Progression

After successfully completing the Apprenticeship, you can progress to the Advanced Apprenticeship. Many employers prefer a beauty therapist to be able to perform at both Level 2 and Level 3. You could then progress into higher education and take a Foundation degree or management qualification. You could also go on to study specialist areas such as massage, aromatherapy, hydrotherapy or reflexology.

There are good career prospects for beauty therapists, such as management of a salon, health farm, spa or leisure club. You could also become a trainer or lecturer, a make-up artist for film and TV or a field sales representative working for a cosmetics or health company. You could even open your own salon.

Carry and deliver goods

This Apprenticeship is designed for those involved in the transport and delivery of goods by light vehicle, van, motorcycle or bicycle.

There are around 10,000 organisations in England and Wales that deal primarily with courier activities, employing over 90,000 people. On this Apprenticeship, you will be working in the logistics sector, which is a vital part of the economy.

Job roles

On this Apprenticeship, you could work as a:

- courier
- delivery van driver
- dispatch rider
- driver's mate.

Work and training

On this Apprenticeship, you will work on the job towards an NVQ Level 2 and off the job towards a BTEC Level 2 Award, both in Carry and Deliver Goods.

Your role will involve multi-drop deliveries, customer interaction and, in some cases, dealing with financial transactions. You will need to work effectively on your own and in a team, observing health, safety and security guidelines. You will develop good customer service skills, complete pre- and post-delivery routines and plan routes and timings for journeys.

As a courier, you would receive pick-up instructions from the depot, collect and sign for items, plan delivery routes and deliver items to addresses. You could be transporting items by van, motorcycle, scooter or, in heavily congested urban areas, bicycle. You may be employed by courier service companies, national delivery firms or licensed mail operators.

As a driver's mate, you would be assisting the driver of a large goods vehicle (LGV), truck or van, travelling with them and helping load and unload deliveries. You could be transporting a wide range of material, from large household items to electrical goods to bulk foodstuffs. You will need to be aware of health and safety issues when moving and storing items. You could be working for a small local firm or a large multi-site distributor.

Entry requirements

There are no minimum entry or previous experience requirements, although you will need to demonstrate that you have the motivation and potential to complete the programme. While you can start this Apprenticeship at the age of 16, employers in practice tend to prefer apprentices to be 17 or above. It helps if you are punctual, reliable, can pay attention to detail and have an interest in driving. You will also need to be able to communicate with a wide range of people and have a good level of fitness.

You will not need to have a full driving licence to start the Apprenticeship as the programme can be completed using a range of vehicles from pedal cycles to large goods vehicles. However, if you are driving a vehicle on your Apprenticeship that requires a licence, you will need to take and pass the appropriate test to complete the Apprenticeship.

Salary once qualified

You could earn from £10,000 to £12,000 on qualification.

Progression

On successful completion of the Apprenticeship, you will become an established operative and there are then a range of progression routes open to you in logistics. You may choose to progress your career by widening your driving skills, for example by becoming an LGV driver. Alternatively, you could move into related areas such as warehouse operations or transport planning. With further experience and qualifications, it is possible to move up into team leading, supervisory and management roles. Some couriers become self-employed.

Facilities management

This Advanced Apprenticeship is designed to provide a career pathway into facilities management. You will be learning all aspects of facilities management and training to become a facilities manager.

You could be working for a large public or private sector organisation or a specialist facilities service company. You could be based at a wide range of buildings from schools and universities to hospitals, offices, shopping centres or sports stadiums.

The sector covers the management of services that support the core activities of an organisation. These can range from property and estates management and building maintenance to catering, cleaning, security, reception and customer care. Facilities managers work behind the scenes to support all these services and ensure a building is operating efficiently, safely and cost-effectively. They are likely to be responsible for a large team of staff.

Job roles
Roles in the sector are:

- assistant facilities manager
- facilities manager.

Work and training
You will work on the job towards Level 3 NVQ Facilities Management and off the job towards Institute of Leadership and Management Level 3 Certificate Facilities Management. You will learn skills specific to facilities management alongside a range of leadership and management skills.

As an apprentice, you could be working as an assistant to a facilities manager or be employed by a facilities management company in a trainee role. You may lead a small team, supervising one or more facilities or services such as cleaning, catering or waste disposal. You will be involved in resolving problems and making sure facilities/services are running smoothly.

Your duties would depend on your employer. You may need to make daily inspections of buildings and equipment to ensure that everything is in working order and fix anything that isn't running correctly. You may also need to check cleanliness and security in the building. You will need to respond to problems as they occur, such as failures of equipment such as the heating system or fire alarm.

You will also be involved in managing resources, staff and budgets as well as managing health and safety at work. You will need to develop working relationships with a wide range of people. Your role may involve liaising with contractors responsible for providing services.

As an apprentice, you can apply for Associate Membership of the British Institute of Facilities Management.

Entry requirements
You will normally be expected to have at least two years' experience in a specialist sector, such as cleaning, catering, customer service, construction or engineering. While employers set their own entry requirements, English and maths at grade C or above are preferred. Some employers may look for five GCSEs at grade C or above.

You will need a strong commitment to customer services and good negotiating, communication and people skills.

Salary once qualified

You could earn around £18,000 after completing the programme.

Progression

On completion of the programme, you could go on to take a Foundation degree in Facilities Management, NVQ Level 4 Facilities Management or another professional qualification.

Apprentices may progress to become assistant facilities managers or facilities managers. With experience, there are good opportunities for progression to senior or regional management posts. Some facilities managers even set up their own consultancy businesses.

Hairdressing

In the UK there are over 35,700 hairdressing salons employing 200,000 people. All salons offer cutting, styling and chemical services. Some offer services to both ladies and men; others specialise in hairdressing for Afro-Caribbean hair and there is a pathway in the apprenticeship framework if you wish to work on this.

You could be working in a salon in a range of locations other than the high street, from hospitals, care homes and prisons to department stores, hotels, airlines and holiday resorts. With qualifications and experience, there are good opportunities to become self-employed and open your own business.

Job roles

At Level 2 (Apprenticeship), you could be a junior stylist.

At Level 3 (Advanced Apprenticeship), roles are:

- hairdresser
- stylist.

Work and training

On the Apprenticeship, you will work on the job towards NVQ Level 2 Diploma in Hairdressing or NVQ Level 2 Diploma in Hairdressing (Combined Hair Types), and on the Advanced Apprenticeship towards NVQ Level 3 Diploma in Hairdressing.

On the Apprenticeship, you will work as a junior stylist, initially helping senior salon staff and working under supervision. Jobs will include advising and consulting with clients, carrying out shampooing and conditioning services, drying and styling hair and mixing and applying chemical treatments. Some apprentices will carry out reception duties, while others will perm hair and provide scalp massage services.

On the Advanced Apprenticeship, you will take responsibility for your own clients. Duties will include:

- cutting, drying, setting, styling and dressing hair using a variety of creative techniques
- advising and consulting with clients
- applying chemical treatments such as perming, relaxing, straightening and colouring
- possibly carrying out additional skills such as Indian head massage or applying hair extensions.

Salary once qualified

You could earn from £10,000 to £16,000 on qualification.

Entry requirements

There are no specific entry requirements, although you will need to have an interest in hairdressing and a good general education. It is an advantage to have had previous work experience in the industry and have three GCSEs in English, maths, science or art, at grade D or above for the Apprenticeship and grade C or above for the Advanced Apprenticeship. It is recommended that you complete the Apprenticeship prior to the Advanced Apprenticeship.

You should have good practical, organisational and verbal communication skills, a high degree of dexterity and good hand–eye co-ordination. It helps to have patience, tolerance and a good sense of humour, as hairdressing relies on repeat business from satisfied customers. You also need to take care with your appearance and be presentable. You will need a high degree of physical stamina.

Progression

From the Apprenticeship, it is possible to enter the Advanced Apprenticeship in Hairdressing as well as other Advanced Apprenticeships in the hair and beauty sector such as the Advanced Apprenticeships in Spa Therapy or in Barbering. From the Advanced Apprenticeship, you can also move on to a Foundation degree in Hairdressing and Salon Management.

There are many opportunities for progression. Junior stylists can progress to become stylists or senior stylists. Stylists can work in salons at home or abroad. You could choose to become self-employed and work on a freelance basis, visiting people in their homes or renting a chair in a salon. With additional training, you could become a technician and specialise in chemical treatments or cutting. There are also opportunities to progress into supervisory or training roles and management or salon ownership. For a few exceptionally talented hairdressers, it is possible to work in film or TV, or as session stylists for magazine photo shoots.

Case Study

Roxanne Moore

Roxanne is on an Apprenticeship in Hairdressing.

'I wasn't sure what I wanted to do when I left school – apart from not working in an office – until I was about 15 years old. I was always playing with my own hair, trying out different styles and colouring it, and then colouring my friends' hair, so I became more interested in hairdressing as a career. Once you've got trained and qualified in hairdressing you'll always have that skill under your belt to fall back on.

'I come into college one day a week and spend the rest of the time as an apprentice in a local salon. I've passed my assessments in blow-drying and putting colours on and am now training in cutting and perming. While you're in training at college, cutting hair for example, you can cut clients' hair but are always supervised, which means you can ask for help if you need it. You are very well supported.

'I'm glad I chose the Apprenticeship rather than the full-time college course as I'm getting real experience of working in a salon, which I think will help me in the long run. Whether I'm cleaning the salon, sweeping up, or making cups of tea, I'm learning what the salon is all about. I've also opened up the salon and dealt with money – counting cheques, cashing up and going to the bank – which gives me a better overview of the business. And I like getting paid as well!

'I'll finish the Apprenticeship next Easter. A good thing with the Apprenticeship is that if you get your head down and organise your assessments and portfolio well you can finish early. I'll finish in April rather than July. I'm not sure whether I'll be taken on after the Apprenticeship because of the current economic climate. If not, I'd be happy to become a mobile hairdresser. I like the idea having some freedom over my hours. Then I might look to rent a chair in a salon. Eventually I'd like to buy my own salon.

'I'm not sure yet whether I'll go on to take the NVQ at Level 3. After getting the NVQ Level 2, it's recommended that you get another year's experience before deciding whether to take the next level or not. I'm looking into doing a short course in nails next, and maybe also a fake tanning course, as these are things I could combine with mobile hairdressing. At the moment, I'm looking forward to working on my own clients in the salon.'

Retail

This sector is very diverse, with retailers selling a vast range of products, from clothing to food to electrical goods. On this apprenticeship, you could be working in anything from a small local shop to a national chain or a large superstore.

Retail is the UK's largest employer outside the public sector. Over three million people currently work in the nation's 300,000 retail businesses.

Job roles

Roles at Level 2 (Apprenticeship) are as follows:

- beauty consultant
- customer service assistant
- fresh food counter assistant (bakery, fish, butchery, fresh produce)
- sales assistant (also called sales associate, sales advisor, sales consultant, retail assistant, retail advisor, general assistant, partner or sales colleague)
- stockroom assistant
- visual merchandiser.

Level 3 (Advanced Apprenticeship) roles are:

- craft expert (e.g. bakery)
- senior sales assistant
- style advisor (personal shopper, retail consultant, stylist)
- store manager of a small outlet
- supervisor, team leader or department manager (also known as floor manager)
- visual merchandiser supervisor.

Work and training

You will develop knowledge and skills specific to your employer and the products and services they offer. On the Level 2 Apprenticeship, you will work on the job towards a Level 2 NVQ in Retail Skills, which will cover everything needed to do the job, and off the job towards a Level 2 technical certificate dealing with essential retail knowledge and understanding.

Many people start their retail career as sales assistants. You will learn customer service, selling skills and product information. You will need to be able to help customers choose the product that is right for them. Your role will vary from retailer to retailer, depending on the product being sold and the amount of assistance the customer requires. In a larger store, you could be working in a specialised department and need expert product knowledge to help with specific enquiries. In a smaller store you will also be expected to help with stock replenishment and keep the sales floor clean and tidy.

As a retail apprentice, your work will include cash handling and putting sales through as well as replenishing and rotating stock. It could also involve putting up displays to encourage people into the store, working in stock control, monitoring stock and placing orders or working on a checkout, making sure payments are properly processed.

On the Advanced Apprenticeship, you will take more responsibility and gain skills needed to progress into management. You can choose from the following pathways.

- Retail management
- Sales professional
- Visual merchandising

You will work on the job towards a Level 3 NVQ in Retail and off the job towards a technical certificate at Level 3. You could cover subjects such as managing customer service, merchandising and sales, stock management, team management and developing people. You could learn a wider range of technical sales skills and start to take on delegated responsibilities such as managing the customer service desk, ordering stock or balancing the tills.

Entry requirements

There are no minimum entry requirements for the Apprenticeship. However, you will need to be interested in retail and show enthusiasm for the retailer and their products and services. Retail is all about service, so it is important that you can communicate effectively and build good relationships. You will need basic numeracy and literacy skills as you will be dealing with money, prices and products. You should also be presentable so you can fit in to the retailer's image and be acceptable to their customers.

For the Advanced Apprenticeship, you may need some GCSEs (at grades A*–C) and/or some experience of working in the service industry.

Salary once qualified

On completing the Apprenticeship, you could earn £11,000 to £15,000.

Progression

In the retail sector, there are good opportunities to progress into supervisory and management positions. On successful completion of the Apprenticeship, you can go on to take the Advanced Apprenticeship, which can lead to middle-management positions. At this level, you would be responsible for a whole store or a department in a superstore. You could then progress to NVQ Level 4 or take a Foundation degree in Retail Management and Leadership.

People progress in management by moving from one store to another or by being promoted to different departments in a larger store. Many corporate retailers run their own in-house management training schemes and these can lead to people running departments, individual stores or a number of stores in a region.

With further training and qualifications there are other opportunities in the sector, in areas such as buying and merchandising, marketing, information technology and financial services.

Warehousing and storage

This Apprenticeship at Level 2 is about the movement and storage of goods in a warehousing operation. Warehousing is a part of logistics operations. Logistics is about the management and movement of goods, from the point of origin to the point of consumption. Warehouses play an important role by storing all kinds of products, from textiles and foodstuffs to chemicals and electrical goods, and then dispatching them to where they are needed.

On the Apprenticeship, you could be working for a wide range of employers, from specialist warehousing and freight companies to supermarkets and retailers, wholesalers, manufacturers and public sector employers. There are around 5,600 workplaces in the UK that deal primarily with warehousing activities.

Job roles

Roles on this Apprenticeship are:

- forklift truck driver
- warehousing operative.

Work and training

On this Apprenticeship, you will work on the job towards a Level 2 NVQ in Warehousing and Storage and off the job towards a Level 2 Certificate in Logistics and Transport or Warehousing and Storage Principles.

As an apprentice, you will gain experience and qualifications as a warehouse operative performing general duties such as the safe movement and storage of goods, either manually or with mechanical assistance (i.e. a forklift truck) and loading goods onto vehicles. You will learn how to work safely and responsibly in a warehouse facility. You may also learn how to handle hazardous goods and materials safely.

You are likely to be involved in dealing with stock of all shapes, sizes and types – including checking deliveries, picking goods up from storage and packaging and despatching products. You will be dealing with customers, colleagues and other people and gain good communication skills. Teamwork skills are also important, as you may be working to a tight schedule while loading and unloading lorries that are waiting to go on to the next job.

Entry requirements

There are no minimum entry or previous experience requirements, although you will need to be able to demonstrate you have the potential to complete the Apprenticeship, are willing to communicate with a range of people and understand the importance of health and safety issues in the workplace.

It helps if you enjoy hands-on, practical tasks, are physically fit, able to cope with paperwork and are computer-literate.

Salary once qualified

After qualification, you could earn around £14,000.

Progression

On successful completion of the apprenticeship, you will become an established warehousing operative. Further progression opportunities reflect a range of career options in a logistics environment, which could include:

- Advanced Apprenticeships in specialised functional areas – e.g. sales, customer service, human resources or team leadership
- Driving Goods Vehicle Advanced Apprenticeship – up-skilling to become a senior LGV driver
- Foundation degree in Logistics
- Traffic Office Advanced Apprenticeship – taking responsibility for the organisation of a delivery, collection or distribution fleet of vehicles.

Alternatively you could take further training and qualifications towards supervisory or management positions.

VEHICLES AND TRANSPORT

This section covers two important sectors vital to vehicles and transport: the retail motor industry and the passenger transport sector. The former is a large and diverse industry employing over half a million people in a wide range of roles. With over 32 million vehicles on the road today, the industry plays a significant part in everyday life. Passenger transport plays an equally important role, delivering crucial services around the UK and helping millions of passengers make journeys by bus, rail, light rail and air. There are over 660,000 people employed in passenger transport in the UK, working in a range of industries and occupations.

As an apprentice in the retail motor industry, you could be working for a car, motorcycle or truck dealership, an independent garage, a vehicle breakdown or rental company, a fast-fit centre or a body repair centre. You may be working for a national chain or a local company. As an apprentice, you could be training to become a vehicle technician, maintaining and repairing all types of vehicles, training in another hands-on role such as body repair, fitting or finishing, or training in vehicle sales. The retail motor industry is a progressive one, with a continuing need for skilled workers. With new models of cars being developed, you could also be working with cutting-edge technology.

In passenger transport, you could be working in a range of industries, including:

- aviation
- bus
- coach
- community transport
- light rail, tram and metrorail
- taxi and private hire.

As an apprentice, you could be working in a variety of occupations, from customer service to operations and engineering. You could be working in ground operations at an airport, for example as an apprentice baggage handler or passenger service agent (looking after passengers), or in rail transport operations training in passenger services, signal operations or control room operations. You may choose to specialise in transport engineering, maintaining and repairing buses and coaches, or learning how to maintain the railway network and rolling stock (rail vehicles).

The skills you need will vary depending on the role and industry you are working in. If you like to use your hands and work with technology, then you may be interested in a technical or engineering role. These require a high level of technical skills, whereas others need 'softer' skills such as customer service.

If you enjoy interacting with customers, you may be interested in working in a customer-facing role, such as passenger services in rail transport operations, which involves tasks such as selling food and drink and answering passenger queries. You would play a crucial role in shaping what passengers think about transport services.

If you are interested in an office-based role and have good organisational skills, then you may be suited to an operations role in passenger transport, working behind the scenes to make everything happen. There are also office-based roles throughout the retail motor industry, as people are needed in finance, marketing, sales, customer service and administration.

You may be interested in a role in these sectors if you:

- enjoy communicating with a range of people
- enjoy working in a team
- have an interest in vehicles and/or passenger transport.

Also, depending on the role, you may:

- have an interest in customer service
- have a friendly and helpful manner
- like persuading people/selling things
- have an interest in technology, science or engineering subjects
- enjoy learning practical skills
- like solving problems
- be good at organising and planning
- enjoy leading a small team.

Apprenticeships are available in the following sectors.

- Aviation operations on the ground
- Passenger-carrying vehicles driving: bus and coach
- Rail services
- Rail transport engineering
- Roadside assistance and recovery
- Transport engineering and maintenance
- Vehicle body and paint operations
- Vehicle fitting
- Vehicle maintenance and repair
- Vehicle parts operations
- Vehicle sales

For information on the relevant Sector Skills Councils, which industries and apprenticeships they represent and web addresses where you can find out more about apprenticeships and careers in this sector, refer to Chapter 9.

Aviation operations on the ground

This Apprenticeship covers ground operations roles at airports. Ground operations keep things running smoothly on the ground and include everything from checking in passengers to maintaining runways and making sure passengers receive their luggage at their final destination.

As an apprentice you could be working in ground operation roles such as passenger service agent, baggage handler and ramp-side operator.

Ground operations staff work at airports throughout the UK. Some are employed by airports or by airlines; however, many are employed by ground handling companies that work on behalf of airlines and airports. These may be large international organisations as well as small regional companies.

The aviation industry is a large employer in the UK. There are 57 commercial airports relying daily on the efficiency of ground operations.

Job roles

Roles in this sector are:

- airfield maintenance
- air-side operations
- baggage handler
- check-in staff
- passenger service agent
- ramp-side operator.

Work and training

On this Apprenticeship, you will learn industry-specific skills. You will work on the job towards the Level 2 NVQ in Aviation Operations on the Ground and off the job towards the Level 2 Certificate in Providing Aviation Operations on the Ground. This will include training in key industry health, safety and security requirements.

As an apprentice passenger service agent, you would be looking after passengers from the time they check in to when they board an aircraft. You would deal with passenger enquiries and help to resolve any problems, which could involve finding alternative travel arrangements.

As an apprentice baggage handler, your role will be to safely and quickly load and unload airline passengers' luggage and cargo to and from the aircraft as well as move it around the airport.

Working in ramp-side operations, you would be learning activities such as turning the aircraft into the correct position for take-off. In airfield maintenance, your work could involve inspecting the runway surface for obstructions such as birds and checking markings and airfield lighting.

Entry requirements

There are no specific academic requirements, although applicants are expected to have GCSEs (A*–C) or equivalent in English and maths. The Diploma in Travel and Tourism may be relevant as well.

It is important that you have an interest in aviation as well as a commitment to a career in the industry. It also helps if you have problem-solving and communication skills and can work well in a team.

In roles that require physical effort, such as baggage handling, applicants have to prove that they are fit and healthy. For passenger-facing roles, it is an advantage to have experience of working in customer service environments, such as call centres, bars, restaurants or shops.

Apprentices aged between 16 and 18 are always employed in a passenger-facing role, due to age restrictions on the use of certain equipment. All applicants for aviation industry roles undergo Criminal Records Bureau checks.

Salary once qualified

After qualification, you could earn £12,000 to £15,000.

Progression

On successful completion of this Apprenticeship, you may choose to broaden your skills further by undertaking additional specialist qualifications at Level 2. You could also progress to the NVQ Level 3 in Co-ordinating Aviation Operations on the Ground.

The Operations on the Ground Apprenticeship leads to entry-level employment. From such a position there are good opportunities to progress into supervisory and management roles.

A baggage handler, for example, could take on ramp responsibilities and become a ramp supervisor. With experience, they could go on to become ground operations managers or move into airport or air-side management. There may also be opportunities to move into other fields of work, such as cargo operations, passenger services and aircraft dispatch. In passenger services, there are also good opportunities to become a team leader or supervisor before moving into planning and management roles.

Rail services

On this Apprenticeship, you will be helping to provide rail services for passengers. You could be working for one of 25 train operating companies, who run services in particular areas or along particular routes. Some run services across the UK, whereas others are more localised. Rail operating companies also manage the majority of railway stations.

The rail industry is a large employer in the UK. With increasing environmental concerns and the rising cost of private cars, use of rail transport is continuing to grow.

Job roles

In this sector, you could work as a:

- conductor
- control room operator

- customer services assistant
- platform assistant
- rail station assistant
- shunter (manoeuvring/parking of train vehicles)
- signal operator
- ticket examiner
- train crew member
- train driver.

Work and training

On this Apprenticeship, you will work on the job towards NVQ Level 2 Rail Operations and off the job towards a Level 2 Award in Rail Services. You will be able to follow one of the following pathways:

- control room operations
- passenger services
- shunting
- signal operations.

On each pathway, you'll learn how to effectively communicate information, work safely and develop and maintain relationships. You will also learn any technical skills relevant to the role.

In passenger services, you will be working in a customer-facing role, such as train driver, on-train crew or station staff. As an apprentice train crew member, you would work on board a train providing services such as selling food and drinks, checking and selling tickets and answering passenger enquiries. As an apprentice rail station assistant, you could be selling tickets, checking tickets at gatelines (i.e. the entries to platforms), providing information to travellers and helping passengers such as wheelchair users to board and disembark.

In some large stations, the role of rail station assistant may be split, with staff taking responsibility for different parts of the station. Roles could include platform assistant, ticket examiner and customer service assistant. Customer service assistants deal with reservations and enquiries and are based in a station information or ticket office.

As an apprentice working in control room operations or signal operations, you would be involved in the background activity of service delivery. This involves planning, controlling and signalling train movements. Control room operators operate and monitor a centralised system to make sure trains are moving safely and running to schedule. Signal operators are responsible for managing the safe movement of trains around the UK. They work in signal boxes and control rooms and use signals to tell drivers when it is safe to proceed.

Entry requirements

There are no standard entry requirements, although employers set their own criteria and will normally look for a basic standard of education, such as GCSEs at grade C or above in

English and maths, or equivalent. You will need to be able to demonstrate an interest in the rail industry and the ability to complete the programme.

Useful skills for rail operations roles include customer service, communication, team working, organisational and planning skills and an awareness of health and safety. For on-train crew and station staff, it helps to have experience of customer service work, for example waiting tables or shop work, and be able to deal confidently with the public.

Salary once qualified

You could earn between £12,000 and £15,000 after your Apprenticeship.

Progression

On successful completion of the Apprenticeship, you may be able to progress to a Level 3 NVQ in Rail Operations, which is designed for either supervisory or technical roles in the industry.

There are good opportunities for internal promotion within train operating companies. On-train and station staff can move into supervisory or team leader positions or into driving roles. Progression is then possible to management and performance-monitoring positions. Signal operators and control room operators can move into signal or control room management or performance management.

If you progress to higher management roles, you will be able to take Level 4 qualifications in operational management or other higher education management qualifications.

Transport engineering and maintenance

On this Apprenticeship, you will be maintaining and repairing buses and coaches or passenger-carrying vehicles (PCVs). You could be working for a large national coach operator, a smaller bus or coach company or possibly a specialist engineering firm.

The road passenger transport industry employs around 156,000 people in 8,000 companies operating bus and coach services across the UK. The coach industry provides charter and scheduled services from day trips and holidays to inter-city journeys. The bus industry provides scheduled transport services in cities, towns and villages across the UK.

Public transport is currently seen as both a cost-effective and attractive means of travel, which has led to increasing numbers of passengers using bus and coach services in recent years.

Job roles

Roles in the sector are:

- auto electrician
- bodywork repairer
- PCV technician.

Work and training

You will work on the job towards a Level 2 NVQ in Transport Engineering Maintenance and off the job towards a relevant technical certificate in transport engineering and maintenance at Level 2. On the Advanced Apprenticeship, you will work towards both a relevant NVQ and a technical certificate at Level 3.

Technicians provide routine maintenance and repairs for a company's buses or coaches. They make sure that buses/coaches are roadworthy and legally compliant and they also carry out any repairs or replacements that may be required if a part has been broken or damaged.

On the Apprenticeship, you will work under supervision in busy bus and coach workshops on a range of vehicle maintenance activities. Initially, you will work on routine maintenance activities such as checks and fault finding, to ensure the vehicle is in good working order. You will use a range of tools and equipment, both hi-tech and hand tools.

With increasing experience, you will become involved in more diagnostic and repair work. If you find a fault, you will work with the senior technicians to identify whether a repair is needed. Any work that you then carry out has to meet with strict industry specifications.

On the Advanced Apprenticeship, you will specialise in mechanical engineering, electrical/electronic engineering or body repair. However, you will generally start by developing the skills required to work in all three areas.

Entry requirements

Recommended entry requirements for the Apprenticeship are three GCSEs, ideally at grade D or above, including maths, English and a science subject. For the Advanced Apprenticeship, you will need either to have completed an Apprenticeship in Transport Engineering Maintenance or have GCSEs at grade C or above in maths, English and a science.

You will also need to have an interest in working with vehicles and be able to demonstrate that you can complete the programme. It also helps if you have a basic understanding of technology, science or engineering, are good with your hands and have sound problem-solving skills.

Salary once qualified

Your salary could be from £14,000 to £17,000 after your apprenticeship.

Progression

After completion of the Apprenticeship, you can progress to the Advanced Apprenticeship and then to a range of further qualifications including supervisory/management training, a Foundation degree or professional institute qualifications.

There is a good progression route for engineering staff. Technicians can progress to skilled technician, senior technician and then master technician or engineer. There are also team leader, supervisory and management roles available with experience.

Engineering managers can take on additional responsibilities for the management of engineering and bus company facilities. It is then possible to move into senior management and director roles.

Vehicle fitting

On this Apprenticeship, you will learn about fast-fit operations in the motor industry. Most fast-fit operations are owned by or affiliated to large tyre manufacturing groups. You are likely to be based in a fast-fit centre, which offers a range of fitting, fast repair and service operations for any make of vehicle.

Job roles

Roles on this Apprenticeship are:

- fast-fit technician
- motor vehicle fitter.

Work and training

On this Apprenticeship, you can choose to specialise in general vehicle fitting, covering the wider aspects of the trade, or specialise in tyre fitting for cars, lorries, buses or plant machinery.

You will work on the job towards a Level 2 NVQ in Vehicle Fitting Operations and off the job towards a relevant technical certificate in vehicle fitting operations at Level 2. The qualifications cover the knowledge you need to get started and the manual skills to do the job. On the Advanced Apprenticeship, you will be working in a supervisory role and aiming at both a relevant NVQ and a technical certificate at Level 3.

Fast-fit technicians, also known as motor vehicle fitters, are responsible for repairing and replacing worn or damaged tyres, exhausts, batteries or parts.

They are normally based in fast-fit centres or in workshops alongside motor vehicle technicians, although some fitters specialise in tractors or other heavy vehicles. As an apprentice working under supervision, your main duties will include:

- testing batteries and other engine parts to find faults
- checking tyres and exhausts for defects.

If you choose to specialise in tyre fitting, you will learn how to remove and replace tyres when they are worn, damaged or faulty. You could be working on all types of vehicles from cars to tractors.

On the Advanced Apprenticeship, you will learn how to supervise fast-fit operations. You would be responsible for supervising repairs to or replacement of worn or damaged tyres, exhausts, batteries or parts. Your main duties will include:

- supporting team members in day-to-day tasks
- testing batteries and other engine parts to find faults
- checking tyres and exhausts for defects.

You will also be managing stock, dealing with customer sales and advising customers.

Entry requirements

Entry requirements for the Apprenticeship vary from employer to employer. However, they will look for a good standard of reading, writing and numeracy and you may need GCSEs in English, maths, science and ICT, or appropriate equivalents.

For the Advanced Apprenticeship, you would normally have completed the Apprenticeship programme and gained the relevant qualifications at Level 2. You will need to have good leadership skills in order to manage a small team of technicians.

You will need to have enthusiasm for the motor industry and a reasonable level of fitness. It also helps if you have:

- the ability to work as part of a team
- good customer service and communication skills
- good manual skills
- the ability to handle cash and credit card transactions.

Salary once qualified

You could earn between £12,000 and £15,000 after completing the programme.

Progression

There is a demand for trained technicians all over the UK. Once qualified, you could work for a fast-fit chain, a franchised dealership owned by manufacturer networks or a privately owned independent garage.

On completion of the Apprenticeship, you can progress to the Advanced Apprenticeship and then on to higher-level qualifications. With experience and qualifications, fast-fit technicians can progress into supervisory and management positions, such as fast-fit supervisor or manager.

There are more opportunities for management roles in large national companies. If you are working for a smaller organisation, you may be able to move into a related area, such as service technician, following training.

Vehicle maintenance and repair

On this Apprenticeship, you could be maintaining and repairing all types of vehicles from motorbikes, cars and vans to larger vehicles such as lorries and coaches. You could be working for a car dealership and focusing on one make of car, or for an independent garage dealing with different makes.

Job roles

Roles on this Apprenticeship are:

- auto electrician
- vehicle technician.

Work and training

On the Apprenticeship, you will work on the job towards a Level 2 NVQ in Vehicle Maintenance and Repair and off the job towards a relevant technical certificate in vehicle maintenance and repair at Level 2. The qualifications cover the knowledge you need to get started and the practical skills for the job. On the Advanced Apprenticeship, you will work towards both a relevant NVQ and a technical certificate at Level 3.

On the Apprenticeship and Advanced Apprenticeship, you can choose between one of the following pathways.

- Auto electrical
- Heavy vehicle
- Light vehicle
- Mobile electronics and security
- Motorcycle

You will specialise in motorcycles, cars, heavy vehicles or electrical systems. You will be trained in all areas of vehicle mechanics and electronics, from engine and exhaust systems to air conditioning and security features. Working in a service technician type role your duties may include:

- servicing old and new vehicles – carrying out checks and maintenance according to the manufacturers' guidelines
- repairing and replacing faulty parts and components.

On the Advanced Apprenticeship, you will learn how to identify and repair more complex faults. You will use diagnostic tools to identify the source of the problem and follow up by making appropriate adjustments and repairs.

Entry requirements

Entry requirements vary between each employer and programme. You will normally need a minimum of three GCSEs, including English and maths at grade C or above. Some places ask for five GCSEs at grade C or above and will vary in which subjects they require.

You will need to have enthusiasm for the motor industry and a reasonable level of fitness. It also helps if you have:

- excellent practical skills
- good communication skills

- the ability to work quickly and have attention to detail
- good problem-solving skills.

Salary once qualified

On completion, you could earn from £13,000 to £15,000.

Progression

There is a demand for trained service technicians all over the UK. Once qualified, you could work for different types of employers such as garages, fast-fit centres, manufacture service centres or vehicle hire and breakdown companies.

Case Study

Charlie Grimmond

Charlie is on an Apprenticeship in Vehicle Maintenance and Repair (Light Vehicle).

'When I was at school, I was initially interested in training to become an electrician, as I'd had some experience of labouring with an electrician at the weekends. But when it came to work experience at school I couldn't find any work experience with an electrician, so found one at a local garage instead. I really enjoyed this and when I was coming up to leaving school I approached the owner of the same garage and asked if he'd take me on as an Apprentice. He offered me an Apprenticeship, and I was really happy to take it.

'I come into college one day a week and spend the rest of my time working at the garage. The garage I work for is fairly big; we work on cars, trucks, and 4x4s. We work on light vehicles, which are those up to seven and a half tonnes. I work on everything – from air conditioning (e.g. replacing pipes and broken compressors) and electrics to general mechanical work and replacing tyres.

'I'm currently working towards NVQ Level 2 in Vehicle Maintenance and Repair (Light Vehicle). I enjoy everything I do at work. I've always enjoyed practical work – my step-dad is a self-employed agricultural engineer and I used to help him on tractors and combines when I was younger.

'At college, I'm working towards a technical certificate, City & Guilds Level 2 Certificate in Vehicle Maintenance and Repair (Light Vehicle). This covers the theory side of vehicle maintenance and repair – for example we have to pass exams in engines, electrics and gearboxes in order to get the qualification. After I've completed the Apprenticeship I'll become a qualified vehicle technician. I'd like to go on to take NVQ at Level 3 as I could then go on to qualify as an MOT technician and take on more challenging work.'

On successful completion of the Apprenticeship, you may progress on to the Advanced Apprenticeship. By developing your level of knowledge, you could move up from a role as a Level 2 service technician to a Level 3 diagnostic technician.

After completing your Level 3 training, you could take further training and qualifications and work your way up to become an MOT tester or a master technician. You may also progress to supervisory or management positions, such as workshop controller, who is responsible for supervising a team of technicians and running the workshop.

It may also be possible to set up your own business and become self-employed.

PART THREE

END NOTE

CHAPTER EIGHT

After your apprenticeship

During your apprenticeship, you will have learned vocational skills and gained valuable qualifications to help you progress in your career.

After you complete your apprenticeship, you may go on to be offered a full-time job by your employer, although if you're not happy you are not obliged to stay with the company that trained you (equally, they can decide to let you go).

In any event, an apprenticeship offers excellent career prospects. You will be able to prove to any employer that you have the required skills and qualifications to do the job. It will therefore give you an edge in the job market and increase your chances of gaining a good rate of pay and promotion.

If you successfully complete an Apprenticeship at Level 2, there may be opportunities to progress on to an Advanced Apprenticeship at Level 3. After completing an Advanced Apprenticeship, and if you enjoy studying, you could choose to progress to higher education. Higher education qualifications can help you gain deeper subject knowledge and increase your progression opportunities further.

You may be able to go on to study for a Foundation degree. These are designed in conjunction with employers to give you skills that you can use immediately in your employment. They can be studied part time so you can continue to work and are work related and work based so they offer a natural progression from an Advanced Apprenticeship. And if you successfully complete a Foundation degree, you can progress on to a full Honours degree.

Many people find they are better suited to work-based learning such as an apprenticeship rather than purely academic learning. With determination, hard work and commitment, it is possible to build a highly successful career from an apprenticeship. In fact, many successful business leaders and high-profile personalities took the vocational learning route and made it to the top of their profession.

Read on to find out more about some of the famous people in the UK who benefited from gaining hands-on skills through apprenticeships.

Famous apprentices

Jamie Oliver

Jamie Oliver left school at the age of 16 to go to Westminster Catering College before training under some leading chefs and going on to become an award-winning chef himself.

Oliver is one of the world's best-loved television personalities and has had huge success with television series such as *The Naked Chef* and *Jamie's School Dinners*. He has also written cookbooks, opened his own restaurants and campaigned against the use of processed foods in national schools.

In 2002, he founded Fifteen. This is a global social enterprise with four restaurants worldwide, all of which operate a pioneering apprenticeship scheme for young people alongside the day-to-day running of the restaurants. Fifteen exists to inspire disadvantaged young people to create great careers in the restaurant industry.

On the Fifteen website, Jamie is quoted as saying, 'Having not been the brightest banana in the bunch myself, I realised that my biggest weapon in life was the determination, enthusiasm, hands-on and "actions speak louder than words" approach my father taught me, and I wanted to get this across to others, especially those interested in food.'

Jamie Oliver was awarded an MBE in 2003 for his contribution to the hospitality industry.

David Beckham

David Beckham signed up as an apprentice with Manchester United in July 1991 at the age of 16. His career started when he made his first-team debut aged 17, before following in the footsteps of his boyhood idol Bryan Robson to become captain of England. He has also become the only England player to score in three different World Cup finals tournaments. Arguably world football's biggest name, David Beckham is also an elite global advertising brand.

Beckham founded a football school called the David Beckham Academy in 2005 in London and Los Angeles. The Academy provides three- or five-day programmes for boys and girls aged from 8 to 15. It also runs a schools programme and, up to 2009, over 10,000 children had taken part in this programme.

In a 2007 interview, Beckham said, 'At school, whenever the teachers asked, "What do you want to do when you're older?" I'd say, "I want to be a footballer." And they'd say, "No, what do you really want to do, for a job?" But that was the only thing I ever wanted to do.'

David Beckham was awarded an OBE in 2003 for services to football.

Alexander McQueen

Alexander McQueen left school at the age of 16 and was offered an apprenticeship at a traditional Savile Row tailors. In less than ten years, he became one of the most respected fashion designers in the world. The skills he learned as an apprentice helped earn him a reputation in the fashion world as an expert in creating an impeccably tailored look.

McQueen worked for some of the top names in fashion before completing a Master's degree in fashion design at Central Saint Martins College of Art and Design. After graduating, his career went from strength to strength. He founded his own label and went on to work with fashion houses such as Givenchy and Gucci. By the end of 2007, McQueen had boutiques in London, New York, Los Angeles, Milan and Las Vegas.

McQueen's hugely successful career brought him numerous awards, including British Designer of the Year four times between 1996 and 2003. He was also awarded a CBE in 2003.

John Frieda

John Frieda started work at the age of 16 as an apprentice with a top Mayfair stylist before going on to become one of Britain's most successful hairstylists in his own right. He was an apprentice to a legendary 70s stylist called Leonard Lewis and quickly became an accomplished editorial stylist. He worked with top models and celebrities on the sets of photo shoots with magazines such as British *Vogue* and *Harpers & Queen*.

He opened his first salon in London, where his elite clientele represented high society, Hollywood stars and royalty. Frieda went on to open more salons but made his fortune from his styling products. In 1988, his first product range debuted in Boots and its key product, Thickening Lotion, was an overnight success. In 1989, he launched Frizz-Ease, which quickly grew into the top-selling line for dry, frizz-prone hair. In the same year, he was named Hairdresser of the Year.

Frieda is now a multimillionaire after founding one of the most successful haircare product companies in the world. He also still retains a number of salons, including two in London and two in New York.

In 2010, Frieda launched HAIRraising, an appeal by the hairdressing industry to collect £1 million towards new operating theatres at Great Ormond Street Hospital. In an interview, he said, 'I'm all or nothing in everything I do. If I'm going to do something, I want it to be effective or successful or I'd rather not do it. Why would you waste your time?'

John Caudwell

John Caudwell left school at the age of 16 to become an apprentice at the local Michelin factory before going on to build a mobile phone empire. In an interview in 2010 he said, 'When I left school, I knew I had to have a solid career behind me. The tyre company Michelin was well respected in my home town of Stoke. It would give me security while I tried to work out how to fulfil my destiny.'

Caudwell did a variety of menial jobs before setting up a corner shop and mail order business. When these failed, he turned to the emerging mobile phone market and registered Midland Mobile Phones.

When he was 21 years old and working as an engineering apprentice at Michelin, Caudwell's weekly wage was £3.50; at the time, the national average was £12. By the time he founded Phones4U in 2000, his Caudwell Group was worth £1 billion. He sold Singlepoint, his air-time reseller, to Vodafone for £405 million. Then in September 2006, he sold the remainder of the group for £1.46 billion.

As you can see from these success stories, an apprenticeship can help you develop your vocational skills and provide you with the right qualifications to help you progress in your career. While not everyone will go on to be a famous chef, footballer, fashion designer or self-made millionaire, an apprenticeship will teach you the habits of dedication and commitment that can help turn your potential into real-life success.

CHAPTER NINE

Further information

Listed in this chapter are web addresses for organisations that can give you further information about apprenticeships, including some that offer online vacancy-matching services and general careers information for all the sectors covered in Chapter 7. This includes information on Sector Skills Councils and standard-setting bodies, and which industries, sector and apprenticeships each one covers.

General information and apprenticeship vacancies

National Apprenticeship Service
- www.apprenticeships.org.uk

The National Apprenticeship Service funds and co-ordinates the delivery of all apprenticeships throughout England. This website has detailed information on apprenticeships in England, including types available by sector, an online vacancy-matching service and a search facility for learning providers.

Department for Employment and Learning
- www.delni.gov.uk/apprenticeshipsni

Information on apprenticeships in Northern Ireland, including details of current frameworks available and a search facility for learning providers.

Careers Wales
- www.careerswales.com

Free careers information and advice for young people, adults, parents and employers in Wales, and an online apprenticeship vacancy-matching service.

MappIT
- www.mappit.org.uk

Information about getting into a Modern Apprenticeship in Scotland, a search facility for learning providers and an online Modern Apprenticeship vacancy-matching service.

The Alliance of Sector Skills Councils Scotland
- www.alliancescotland.org

Information on Modern Apprenticeships, including details of the current frameworks available. The Alliance of Sector Skills Councils Scotland represents the work of the Sector Skills Councils in Scotland.

Alliance of Sector Skills Councils
* www.sscalliance.org

Links on the website to each Sector Skills Council. The Alliance of Sector Skills Councils represents the 25 UK councils.

Engineering Connections
* www.apprentices.co.uk

Engineering apprenticeship recruitment site where you can search for engineering apprenticeship vacancies in your region and apply online.

Sector Skills Councils and standard-setting bodies

Business, administration, finance and ICT

The Council for Administration
* www.cfa.uk.com

The Council for Administration is the standard-setting organisation for business skills. Visit this website for information on apprenticeships relevant to business and administration skills.

The Financial Services Skills Council
* www.fssc.org.uk

This is the Sector Skills Council for the finance sector. Visit the website for information on apprenticeships and careers in finance, accountancy and financial services.

e-skills UK
* www.e-skills.com

This is the Sector Skills Council for business and information technology. Visit www.e-skills.com/apprenticeships for information on apprenticeships in the sector, and www.e-skills.com/careers for information on career opportunities and the skills required for a career in ICT and telecommunications.

Construction and the built environment

ConstructionSkills
* www.bconstructive.co.uk

ConstructionSkills is the Sector Skills Council for construction. Visit bConstructive for information on apprenticeships and careers in the industry.

Summit Skills
* www.goodday.org.uk/careers

Summit Skills is the Sector Skills Council for the building services engineering sector. Visit the website for information on apprenticeships and careers in this sector.

Creative industries

Creative and cultural skills
- www.ccskills.org.uk and www.creative-choices.co.uk

Creative and Cultural Skills is the Sector Skills Council for the craft, cultural heritage, design, music, literature and performing and visual arts industries. Visit www.ccskills.org.uk for information on apprenticeships and www.creative-choices.co.uk for general information on careers in the creative industries and cultural sector.

Skillset
- www.skillset.org

Visit this website for information on the Advanced Apprenticeship in Creative and Digital Media, the Apprenticeship in Fashion and Textiles and the apprenticeship in Photo Imaging.

Skillset is the Sector Skills Council for creative media, which comprises advertising, animation, computer games, film, interactive media, photo imaging, publishing, radio and television and fashion and textiles. For general information on careers in these sectors, visit www.skillset.org/careers

Energy and utilities

Energy & Utility Skills (EU Skills)
- www.euskills.co.uk

Energy & Utility Skills is the Sector Skills Council for the gas, power (excluding nuclear), waste management and water industries. Visit this website for information on apprenticeships and careers in these areas.

Cogent
- www.cogent-ssc.com

Cogent is the Sector Skills Council for the chemicals, pharmaceuticals, nuclear, oil and gas, petroleum and polymer industries. Visit this website for information on careers in these industries and information on the Apprenticeship in Nuclear Decommissioning and the Apprenticeship in Specialised Process Operations (Nuclear).

Engineering and manufacturing technologies

Cogent
- www.cogent-ssc.com

As well as general information on careers in the chemicals, pharmaceuticals, nuclear, oil and gas, petroleum and polymer industries, Cogent also provides details of the Apprenticeship in Process Technology and the Apprenticeship in Polymer Processing and Signmaking.

Improve

- www.improveltd.co.uk

Improve is the Sector Skills Council for the food and drink manufacturing industry. Visit this website for information on the apprenticeship in Food Manufacture and for careers in the food and drink industry.

The British Marine Federation

- www.britishmarine.co.uk

The British Marine Federation is the trade association for the leisure and small commercial marine industry. Visit this website for information on the Marine Industry Apprenticeship and careers in this area.

Proskills

- www.proskills.co.uk and www.prospect4u.co.uk

The Sector Skills Council for the process and manufacturing sector, Proskills covers building products, extractives, coatings, wood, paper, print, furniture, glass, and glazed ceramics. For information on apprenticeships in this sector, visit www.proskills.co.uk, and for information on careers, visit www.prospect4u.co.uk

Semta

- www.semta.org.uk

Semta is the Sector Skills Council for science, engineering and manufacturing technologies. Its website offer information on apprenticeships and careers in engineering and details of the Apprenticeship for Laboratory Technicians.

Environmental and land-based industries

Lantra

- www.lantra.co.uk and www.afuturein.com

Lantra is the Sector Skills Council for environmental and land-based industries. For information on apprenticeships in these areas visit www.lantra.co.uk, and for careers in the sector visit www.afuturein.com

Health, public services and care

Skills for Health

- www.skillsforhealth.org.uk

Skills for Health is the Sector Skills Council for the health sector. Visit this website for information on relevant apprenticeships.

Skills for Care & Development
- www.skillsforcareanddevelopment.org.uk

Skills for Care & Development is the Sector Skills Council for people working in early years, children and young people's services and social care. Visit this website for further information and links to relevant organisations providing information on careers and apprenticeships in these areas.

Lifelong Learning UK (LLUK)
- www.lluk.org

LLUK is the Sector Skills Council for people working in the lifelong learning sector. Visit this website for information on Apprenticeships in Advice and Guidance; Community Development; Information and Library Services; Youth Work.

Skills for Justice
- www.skillsforjustice.com

This is the Sector Skills Council for the justice sector; its website offers information on the Advanced Apprenticeships in Community Justice and Emergency Fire Operations.

Skills for Security
- www.skillsforsecurity.org.uk

Skills for Security is the skills body for the security industry, and its website offers information on relevant apprenticeships.

The Training and Development Agency for Schools
- www.tda.gov.uk

The Training and Development Agency for Schools is the sector body responsible for training and developing the schools workforce. Visit this website for information about the Apprenticeship in Supporting Teaching and Learning in Schools, and general careers information on school support staff.

Asset Skills
- www.assetskills.org

Asset Skills is the Sector Skills Council for facilities management, housing, property, planning, cleaning and parking. Visit its website for information on careers in these industries and on the Apprenticeship in Housing.

Hospitality, leisure, travel and tourism

People 1st

- www.people1st.co.uk and www.uksp.co.uk

People 1st is the Sector Skills Council for hospitality, leisure, travel and tourism. Information about apprenticeships in this sector is available on its website at www.people1st.co.uk, and further information on careers, qualifications and training is available on the dedicated careers site www.uksp.co.uk.

SkillsActive

- www.skillsactive.com/careers

This is the Sector Skills Council for the active leisure, learning and well-being sector. The website offers further information on apprenticeships, careers, qualifications and training in this sector.

GoSkills

- www.goskills.org and www.careersinpassengertransport.org

GoSkills, the Sector Skills Council for passenger transport, offers information on cabin crew apprenticeships at www.goskills.org and general careers information on the aviation industry at www.careersinpassengertransport.org.

Retail and commercial enterprise

Skills for Logistics

- www.deliveringyourfuture.co.uk and www.skillsforlogistics.org

Skills for Logistics is the Sector Skills Council for the freight logistics industry. The above websites provide information on apprenticeships and careers in the sector.

Habia

- www.habia.org

Habia is the standard-setting body for the hair, beauty, nail, spa, barbering and Afro-Caribbean hair industries. For further information on apprenticeships and careers in these industries, visit the website.

Skillsmart Retail

- www.skillsmartretail.com

Skillsmart Retail is the Sector Skills Council for retail. Visit its website for information on the Apprenticeship in Retail and details of careers in the sector.

Asset Skills

- www.assetskills.org

Asset Skills, the Sector Skills Council for facilities management, housing, property, planning, cleaning and parking, offers information on careers in these industries on its website, and on Apprenticeships in Property Services; Facilities Management; Cleaning and Support Services; Surveying.

Vehicles and transport

The Institute of the Motor Industry

- www.motor.org.uk/careers

The Institute of the Motor Industry is the Sector Skills Council for the automotive retail industry, and its website offers further information on apprenticeships and careers in this area.

GoSkills

- www.goskills.org and www.passengertransport.org

GoSkills is the Sector Skills Council for passenger transport. For information on apprenticeships in this sector visit www.goskills.org, and for information on careers in this sector visit www.careersinpassengertransport.org.